The Path
to Spiritual
Advancement

ALSO BY DR. DAVID R. HAWKINS, M.D., Pн.D.

Book of Slides:
The Complete Collection Presented at the 2002–2011
Lectures with Clarifications

Daily Reflections from Dr. David R. Hawkins:
365 Contemplations on Surrender, Healing,
and Consciousness

Discovery of the Presence of God: Devotional Nonduality

The Ego Is Not the Real You:
Wisdom to Transcend the Mind and Realize the Self

The Eye of the I: From Which Nothing Is Hidden

Healing and Recovery

The Highest Level of Enlightenment:
Transcend the Levels of Consciousness for
Total Self-Realization

I: Reality and Subjectivity

In the World, But Not of It:
Transforming Everyday Experience into a Spiritual Path

Letting Go: The Pathway of Surrender

The Letting Go Guided Journal:
How to Remove Your Inner Blocks to Happiness,
Love, and Success

The Map of Consciousness Explained:
A Proven Energy Scale to Actualize Your Ultimate Potential

Power vs. Force:
The Hidden Determinants of Human Behavior

Reality, Spirituality and Modern Man

Success Is for You:
Using Heart-Centered Power Principles for Lasting Abundance
and Fulfillment

Transcending the Levels of Consciousness:
The Stairway to Enlightenment

Truth vs. Falsehood: How to Tell the Difference

The Wisdom of Dr. David R. Hawkins:
Classic Teachings on Spiritual Truth and Enlightenment

Please visit:

Hay House USA: www.hayhouse.com®
Hay House Australia: www.hayhouse.com.au
Hay House UK: www.hayhouse.co.uk
Hay House India: www.hayhouse.co.in

The Path to Spiritual Advancement

How to Transcend the Ego and Experience the Presence of God

David R. Hawkins, M.D., Ph.D.

HAY HOUSE LLC

Carlsbad, California • New York City

London • Sydney • New Delhi

Published in the United States by: Hay House LLC: www.hayhouse.com®
Published in Australia by: Hay House Australia Publishing Pty Ltd:
www.hayhouse.com.au
Published in the United Kingdom by: Hay House UK Ltd: www.hayhouse.co.uk
Published in India by: Hay House Publishers (India) Pvt Ltd:
www.hayhouse.co.in

Project editor: Sally Mason-Swaab
Cover design: Jordan Wannemacher
Interior design: Lisa Vega

The original titles of the audio lecture series are *Causality: The Ego's Foundation* and *Radical Subjectivity: The "I"of Self.*

Cataloging-in-Publication Data is on file at the Library of Congress

Tradepaper ISBN: 978-1-4019-7706-1
E-book ISBN: 978-1-4019-7707-8

10 9 8 7 6 5 4 3 2 1
1st edition, July 2024

Printed in the United States of America

This product uses responsibly sourced papers and/or recycled materials.
For more information, see www.hayhouse.com.

CONTENTS

✳✳✳

INTRODUCTION

* ✳ *

Dr. David R. Hawkins wanted to present a series of 12 lectures that would be the basis of his spiritual work and add further detail to the significant writings covered in *Power vs. Force*. He had discovered that by using the simple muscle-testing method, he could inquire into the nature of Consciousness itself, and after completing over 20 years of consciousness research, his book *Power vs. Force* was published in 1995. This book opened the door to discovering more enlightening information, new truths, and stimulating questions; the response from so many people from all walks of life was awe-inspiring and revealing.

People asked for more. Dr. Hawkins realized that Consciousness itself continued to grow and evolve, and as a spiritual teacher dedicated to the highest Truth, to God, and to his love for humanity, he decided to give the lecture presentations.

Including his ongoing research, Dr. Hawkins created visual aids and graphs that featured his famous Map of Consciousness® chart and presented his findings with great clarity and purpose. His lighthearted spirit, wonderful sense of humor, and real-life stories graced all who attended these lectures. With his wife, Susan, as his assistant and a caring presence onstage, the 2002 lectures came to be and are the core of Dr. Hawkins's body of work that he later called "the Pathway of Devotional Nonduality." Each lecture begins and ends with this high statement: *Gloria in excelsis deo* ("glory to God in the Highest").

In your hands is the first book of a six-book series. It comprises the transcribed lectures 1 and 2 presented in January and February 2002 by Dr. Hawkins. We have kept the transcriptions as pure and as close to Dr. Hawkins's voice as possible but have deleted redundancies and grammatical inconsistencies.

As you read, you will learn about:

Part I

▲ The Map of Consciousness® chart from 0 to 1,000 and how it came to be

▲ The evolution of consciousness and the importance of level 200

▲ The limitations of the Newtonian paradigm and the description of quantum physics

▲ The illusion of causality: the great block to spiritual advancement

▲ Transcending the ego through understanding and recontextualizing it

▲ How one can move up the levels of Consciousness through spiritual intention and choice

▲ The purpose of Dr. Hawkins's work: to realize the Presence of God

Part II

▲ Radical subjectivity, the essence of experiencing the Presence of God as "I"

▲ How the spiritual realm is based on context and is a different paradigm

▲ The role of karma in a person's life

▲ Existence vs. nonexistence: the great conundrum that Dr. Hawkins faced

▲ The Power of Divinity: there is only one variable

▲ How one surrenders the ego to God: through Radical Honesty

These are just a few of the many topics that Dr. Hawkins discusses in this book. It can be a companion to the actual lectures in video or audio format by Dr. Hawkins, or a standalone reading that will inspire and encourage you along your spiritual path.

Dr. Hawkins tells us that we are safe and to trust our safety in the Truth and Loving Presence of Divinity itself. We hope this book gives you a sense of that love and safety and spur you onward and upward.

Blessings,

Veritas Publishing Staff

▲

PART I

Causality:
The Ego's Foundation

MAP OF CONSCIOUSNESS®

God-view	Life-view	Level		Log	Emotion	Process
Self	Is	Enlightenment	⇧	700-1000	Ineffable	Pure Consciousness
All-Being	Perfect	Peace	⇧	600	Bliss	Illumination
One	Complete	Joy	⇧	540	Serenity	Transfiguration
Loving	Benign	Love	⇧	500	Reverence	Revelation
Wise	Meaningful	Reason	⇧	400	Understanding	Abstraction
Merciful	Harmonious	Acceptance	⇧	350	Forgiveness	Transcendence
Inspiring	Hopeful	Willingness	⇧	310	Optimism	Intention
Enabling	Satisfactory	Neutrality	⇧	250	Trust	Release
Permitting	Feasible	Courage	⇕	200	Affirmation	Empowerment
Indifferent	Demanding	Pride	⇩	175	Scorn	Inflation
Vengeful	Antagonistic	Anger	⇩	150	Hate	Aggression
Denying	Disappointing	Desire	⇩	125	Craving	Enslavement
Punitive	Frightening	Fear	⇩	100	Anxiety	Withdrawal
Disdainful	Tragic	Grief	⇩	75	Regret	Despondency
Condemning	Hopeless	Apathy	⇩	50	Despair	Abdication
Vindictive	Evil	Guilt	⇩	30	Blame	Destruction
Despising	Miserable	Shame	⇩	20	Humiliation	Elimination

CHAPTER 1

The Calibrations: An Introduction

I am very pleased to share with you the first in a series of 12 lectures. Over the last 20 years, the [consciousness] research has advanced considerably. My book *Power vs. Force* was preceded by a good 10 years of research, and to make sure that it met the scientific criteria of today's world, I went to the bother of getting a Ph.D. so as to give it greater academic credence.

The purpose of *Power vs. Force* was to go from the familiar linear world and provide a context in which you could move into the less familiar and nonlinear with some degree of comfort that you're not moving into the purely mystical, imaginary realms. So, I was presenting it from the viewpoint of whom I considered the average intelligent reader who is also interested in spirituality and who is focused on the parameter, the leading edge, of advanced theoretical physics—which is stuck right now because it can't get beyond this block between the linear and nonlinear domains. It's gone about as far as it can go in the linear domain.

I was hoping to enlarge the paradigm of the reality of science so that the intelligent reader could comprehend the work and say, "There must be something in the nonlinear domain that we should be looking at." So, that was that purpose. The purpose of *Power vs. Force* was to take us from the familiar, the Newtonian paradigm of reality, and prepare us that there is evidence; evidence of the reality of the nonlinear, because that's the great learning block.

The intellectuals at the time constantly used the term *evidence based*. Anything having to do with the nature of man was no longer relevant, and we could only talk about white mice, levers, and doses of meds and neurotransmitters. No mention of anything human was allowed, because everything had to be "evidence based."

Well, the purpose of *Power vs. Force* was to provide evidence-based data. It introduced the Map of Consciousness®, which has become relatively well-known and has been reprinted in many, many other books and cited in many references. What I tried to do was present evidence-based documentation of the reality of the nonlinear domain and provide some kind of signposts so that the unfamiliar could be approached without undue anxiety. People who think the only world is the intellectual world of logic or the material world are rather frightened of anything that goes beyond their paradigm. It has to do with paradigm anxiety. That there's anything real that is beyond science's capacity to measure is rather scary to many people, and they vociferously get on television. You see them at night, trying to prove that near-death experiences are all due to brain physiology, and God is probably just a nucleus in the hypothalamus somewhere—trying to keep reality confined to this box of the logical and comfortable. And there are some people whose lives are devoted to knocking anything beyond the ordinary paradigm.

So, *Power vs. Force* was, then, the introduction to the material, and the thing that was interesting about it is that we learned that you can't use ordinary mechanical instruments when you're dealing with the nonlinear. The nonlinear has to do with life itself. Consequently, it would seem obvious that the measuring instrument of that domain would be a living thing; in this case, a human being—and the response of that human being to the field of consciousness.

Once in a while, I get a letter from a reader that says, "Can't you somehow do this electronically?" That's missing the point altogether. No, you cannot do that electronically; nor would I have any interest in doing it, because that is a different world. The electronically recordable world is the Newtonian paradigm of reality, which, according to our calibrated levels of consciousness, stops at 499.

We can follow the greatest scientific minds in history—Newton and Freud and Einstein—and we push the limits of the scientific, logical mind. And on our scale of consciousness, with which most people are familiar, 499 is pretty much the edge of the Newtonian paradigm. You'll find a lot of very advanced theoretical scientific theses, et cetera, and doctrines and bodies of knowledge stop at 499. It's amazing how over the centuries, so many—Sir Francis Bacon—so many of them stop at 499. At first, I thought I was making a mistake here. How can they all be 499? There were some I could not believe were 499, like Einstein. I said, "No, he's got to be more than 499." But no, it was 499. So, that's pretty much the level at which we begin to emerge into a different paradigm of reality.

Power vs. Force took us, then, from the Newtonian into the nonlinear—from the linear domain to the nonlinear. You see, if we use language that is not religiously, historically loaded, you get a wider audience. If you mention it in spiritual or religious terms, dealing in Sanskrit terms, a number of people will stop reading, for one reason or another. So, I have tried to stick with primarily common wording, and so the world of familiarity. America calibrates right now at 421. That's the intellect. The 400s are the intellect. So, anybody who is reasonably intellectually curious would find the work interesting, and it would lead them to the door of a new discovery.

Right in the beginning, I want to correct sort of a misconception that may have arisen, and it also has to do with the advancement of my own consciousness and understanding. We developed a calibrated Map of Consciousness®, at which 200 was a critical level. We found that everything above 200—everything that's true, everything that's valid, everything that's pro-life, everything that's spiritually whole—goes from 200 up and makes you go strong. Everything below 200 makes you go weak. And it goes all the way down to the bottom. So, the very top of the scale of consciousness is 1,000—Jesus Christ, Krishna, Buddha—the Great Avatars that have set the paradigm of spiritual reality for thousands of years, calibrated at 1,000. And at that time, we discovered by asking that the human nervous system cannot tolerate spiritual energy beyond 1,000. And those of you who have gone into very advanced states of consciousness will remember that up to 600 is extremely pleasant. In the high 500s, it gets ecstatic. Everything is incredibly beautiful; the sound is crystalline and pure; there's a total oneness to everything; everything happens by synchronicity. If you think *salt*, somebody says, "Would you like some salt?" It's a marvelous world. You can leave in the high 500s, you can walk out of the door without a nickel in your pocket and no food, and everything will be provided, and I've done it. I walked out without anything and, just as you think, *Gosh, I could sure use a snack*, a friend of yours says, "I'm going for breakfast, I'm going to take you out for breakfast." It just happens that way, and you can go for months without anything at all. So, the high 500s are the world of the synchronous, the miraculous, harmonious—it's an exquisite world. Many gurus, I would say the majority that the world considers to be gurus, are in the mid-to-high 500s. Over 540, as you remember, is Unconditional Love.

People ask me, "What's a true guru?" A true guru (and we asked with kinesiology) has to calibrate over 540: Unconditional Love.

So, that brings us up to 600. The ride up to 600 is hard work in the beginning, but after a while, it becomes intensely inspired, and it takes on an energy of its own. And the movement, the spiritual movement, continues of its own volition, you might say. It's like the spiritual energy is so strong that it now takes over the whole process, and you become more of a witness of it. At 600, one reaches a state that the world calls enlightened, in which you may or may not stay in the world. You may or may not stay in the world. At 600, everything sort of goes into a state of exquisite bliss, and it's very difficult to function. It's questionable whether or not to even breathe. A number of times, breathing only resumed because somebody insisted on it, but you didn't need to breathe, and that state was perfect. The body disappears as a reality, and there is really no reason to continue. However, there's probably a karmic propensity, a momentum that carries one along. In each instant that that happened, it was Love that got the body to breathe again. So, Love for someone who would have been concerned if the body stopped breathing—the world considers that death and goes into a great "reaction" about that. Somebody that you care about, you look at him and you realize he believes in death and he thinks you're dead, and he will now feel very bad about that, so you breathe. That's the only reason you breathe, because you really don't have to.

At that point, one has really entered a nonlinear domain. At 700, we're going to redo a few things. We don't have anything from 700 to 1,000, except it just says, "Enlightenment." Actually, Enlightenment starts at 600. At 700, the reality of the Self, with a capital *S*, is All That Is. Those are the levels of Ramana Maharshi, Nisargadatta Maharaj, swamis—a number of them. Eight hundred is quite a higher level, and up to 600 is blissful and maybe even close to 700, but beyond that, the trip, at least in this case, was extremely painful.

The slightest thing that's "out" brings a wracking pain through the whole nervous system. It was horrific at times, and by meditation and prayer, one gets what the paradox is that's blocking you. So, you learn that what the world considers to be *the* state is one of a series of states. Although it's true that enlightenment is at 600, most people at 600 don't move any further. Half of them leave the world and don't return, go into retirement, withdraw from the world—or, I suppose, there was nobody around to cajole them into breathing, so they didn't.

Seldom do they move beyond that. First of all, the state is so complete and total and satisfying that there would be no thought to move beyond. There is no beyond. You are already at the ultimate state; 600 is already an ultimate state, so there's nowhere to move beyond, nor is there any reason to do so. Once in a great while, peculiarly, that state will begin to move of its own. That inner drive of the Self within, an aspect of Consciousness itself, presents a paradox, because 600 isn't the solution of every paradox that's possible. And a paradox will appear, and with it, this wracking physical pain. One then intuits what the paradox is, or it just comes to you as you're driving along. And these are dualities that are extremely abstract and that are not worth bothering with for the average person.

The Paradox: Existence vs. Nonexistence

Those of you who know my personal story know that my spiritual sojourn began at age three. When I was complete nothingness, suddenly there was a shocking awareness of existence. I had returned into actual existence. The paradox then that arose—at age three, there was no mentation, but there was a complete and total understanding of the paradox. There came the fear of nonexistence. To exist brings up its polar opposite of nonexistence. And the fear came up: if I had come into existence, then it might have been that I would *not* have come into existence. So, the paradox to be solved in this lifetime, which only took another 50 years to solve—or 60 years, or whatever—was existence versus nonexistence. To solve that paradox takes you beyond what? Let's see what "existence versus nonexistence" is. "Existence versus nonexistence comes up as a blockade at 800" (calibrates True); "810" (True); "840" (Not true); "830" (True); "835" (Not true). It comes up at 835. So, at consciousness level 835 comes up this incredible pain, and that paradox of existence versus nonexistence is—the question is really: Is there an opposite to God? And the answer is no. Is there an opposite to existence? No. So, it's a very high paradox, but you don't have to worry about it until then. That's good news.

The bad news is, if you have the karmic momentum to continue on after having reached such a blissful state, you go through some agonizing states.

An example of this is when we were in Korea in 2001, and I was in such an agonizing state. I forget what that polarity was. You see, consciousness is blocked all the time by a positionality, which we'll get into. Positionality creates a duality. Well, there are dualities within the ordinary domain—Love and hate, and all that everybody's familiar with. But there are paradoxical, seeming dualities at much higher levels, but you don't have to really bother with them until you get there. So there I was, wracked with pain, and I was intuiting what it was and sort of meditating, and then suddenly, I saw it. It was extremely painful, like your whole body is on fire. It's like your nervous system is made up of barbed wire, and the barbed wire now has electricity running through it. It is a wracked pain. It is really within the whole aura. You can't get away from it, because it's the aura that does that. In other words, it demands attention. So, I was questioning why that is. And Susan was reading something out of—there was a Buddhist bible in Korea, in the hotel room—in it, she was reading that the Buddha was wracked with pain, as though his bones were broken, and he was attacked by demons. She read that to me, and instantly I felt better. It's okay to be wracked by demons and feel like all your bones are broken. So those are just adventure stories, neither here nor there.

What I was really driving at is, out of *Power vs. Force*, there seemed to arise (and it bothered me at the time) a seeming duality, or at least one could draw a sort of political position about it. Above 200 is that which is pro-life, supports life, and that which is true. Below 200 is that which is not true, does not support life; everything that is venomous, hateful, selfish, greedy, and destructive to others. That seemed to create a certain polarity. So, here is the work devoted to transcending polarities, and the work itself seems to be bringing up a polarity—similar to good and evil. There is above 200 and below 200. And below

200, keep away from them: "Don't go out and play with those kids that are below 200, Jimmy. They have wicked, greedy thoughts and are out to drag you down into a street gang, and get you tattooed and drugged up and hooked on heroin or something." And to lure you into crime or evil. So, it seemed to create that, and that bothered me, and yet we went back over and over it again. Of course, those of you who are familiar with the work and have done kinesiology yourself know it is extremely definite. There's nothing imaginary. If science wants evidence-based work, kinesiology is truly evidence based. Your arm either goes strong or it goes weak. And there is no if, and, or but about it. And it always gives you the same answer.

Creation Is Continuous

And then it dawned on me that, first of all, the scale is drawn a little incorrectly, and I want to redraw it today. The other thing is that it's not really two different worlds. What happens is this: Near the top of the scale at 1,000, you have the Great Avatars, so there's the universal Presence. There's the Unmanifest, which becomes manifest as creation. Creation is continuous. Consciousness, as it interacts with matter, evolves as life. And then life evolves up into higher and higher capacities through evolution. Therefore, creation and evolution are one and the same thing. What science calls evolution is nothing but the unfolding of creation. As creation unfolds sequentially, perception thinks it sees something happening. It's only the unfolding of evolution. So, evolution is nothing but a demonstration of the fact that creation is continuous. This gets us away from the view that God was around at the time of Genesis; He created the world and took off.

And you don't see Him again until you get to heaven. So, God is elsewhere in time, way back in the early, early beginning—prehistoric—and you're not going to see Him unless you've been very, very good, and you go to a heavenly place where He sits waiting in judgment. Oh my god, what a scary paradigm of reality. In the meantime, you're on your own, folks.

Once in a while, He says strange things to people, who sometimes get put in mental hospitals for what He says. Or He speaks through prophets and various bizarre pronouncements. So, it's a strange world. And of course, it explains why most people never find God. If He was way in prehistoric times and does not exist until you get to heaven, you're pretty much on your own.

But the reality of it is that that which shines forth as Divinity is the pure essence out of which arises Love. And this Love then does radiate down throughout creation, much like the proverbial step-down transformers. And, if you calibrate the level of an archangel—let's just do it for fun: "An archangel—we have permission: resist—" (True), "—runs 500,000 and over: resist" (True). Okay. Now this is a logarithmic scale, folks, and every step as you get higher and higher is an enormous increase of energy. And an archangel runs 500,000 and up. So, we're talking about power of such immensity. When I first witnessed it and went into that state—the power that holds rock together, steel together, holds the planet together, holds the universe together, is the infinite power of God, which we think is physical; we witness it as physical—that is the power of God. The cohesion between atoms and what makes cement hard is the infinite power of God, is manifesting in that domain.

This enormous power, then, the Light. So, Genesis calibrates positive. There's only three books in the Old Testament, and Genesis is one of them, that calibrates positive. In the Old Testament, you have Psalms, Proverbs, and Genesis, the only three books in the Old Testament that test positive. So, this infinite power then radiates forth as the light of Love. Here's what we're actually seeing [on the board] is that the top—the amount of Love is high at the top of the scale and becomes less and less. If this picture was drawn correctly, the lower half of the scale as we get below 200—the top would be very bright, and then it darkens as we go down, and as we go below 200, it gets darker and darker, and by the bottom of the scale, it's pretty black.

So, what we're seeing, then, is not "good" and "evil"; this is not two contrasting either/ors. You're seeing a great deal of Love, less and less and less Love, and it diminishes. You're looking more like at a thermometer, you see? There's only one variable. Don't forget, to get beyond dualities, you have to realize the error is assuming that there're two variables. There's only one variable, and we will explain that. There's either light—the only variable between light and darkness is, there's only light. There aren't two things, such as "light" and "darkness." There's only light. Light is either there, or it's not there. The light can be very bright, or it can be very, very dim. When it gets very, very dim, we say it's darkness. Darkness is not a thing. You can't shine darkness into a closet and shine me some darkness. It has no reality, the absence of light. So there's only one variable, and that's light. In the scale of consciousness, then, there's only one variable, and that's Love. Infinite Love makes you infinitely powerful.

My moment of Enlightenment, which was January 10, 1965, left me jarred and thoughtless for many years. Recently, out of curiosity—I was almost too scared to ask, "That one was the one at 500,000: resist" (True). "It was a thought from the one at 500,000: resist" (True). A thought—out of enormous prayer, an archangel merely gives you a thought, an instant—took me right out of the world, of what the world calls reality, into a different, total reality.

Therefore, analogous to light, then, the top of the scale at 1,000 is about as much light as protoplasm can handle without frying. And it fries even there. So, this light is very intense, and the ordinary protoplasm really cannot handle it. It scales down then, and we notice that, at what we calibrate at 200, what has happened here is that you haven't gone from Love to not-Love. What's happened is that it changes quality. Now, in any progression of comparisons, you'll notice the logical error was made by Aristotle—and was made by all the great thinkers of all time—in looking for the primary "cause."

Let's say, in St. Thomas Aquinas's arguments for the existence of God, there is the classic argument of "first cause." We're going to try and get rid of "cause." It's a great impediment. Don't forget that we have to eliminate "cause" from our thinking!

It gets down to "first cause." The difficulty with that kind of thinkingness is that it doesn't realize that many sequences; there's a change of quality along the way, which they don't take into account—a change of quality. As you look through a sequence at what the world calls "causes," you're expecting to find something that's very, very similar as cause number Uno. Cause number Uno is of a different quality. The same thing, you'll understand as soon as I tell you this, if we take a thermometer—let's say, above 1,000, the water turns into steam. When you get down to calibration level 200, it turns to ice. It is still only H$_2$O, but whoa, what a change of quality. So, what we have at 200 is not a duality of water versus non-water; we just have, at this end, hot water—Jesus and Krishna and all those people—and then at 200, this water turns into ice. It's still just water. It is not a duality of water versus non-water. Okay? That will help a lot of people. You see, when you get caught by the dualities, which is created by some positionality, the way you transcend perception is, you have to find the positionality that's creating that duality and remove that positionality, and the duality then collapses. What you see is that Reality is not a duality; it's a gradation. Let's say, "good" and "evil"—you could start with "good" at the top, and then remove more and more "good," and at a certain point, depending on what your positionality is, you would say, "Well, that's 'evil.'" Well, people would be in different places.

I treat a lot of street kids. I am in a girls' ranch. We have lots of juvenile adolescents there. And their scale of what's okay and what's not okay is quite a bit different than what goes on at Harvard—or what goes on in the Lower East Side in New York City. Anyway, to them, what we would consider really malevolent, to them it would just be a kick. Not only that, but they have a rationale that they asked for it. Their position is, if your purse gets stolen, "Well, she asked for it; she left it on the back of her chair in the store. I mean, what do you expect?" So that's their idea of good and evil: "It's her fault because she left the purse sitting there." They believe that that's true. "It's not wrong to steal. She left her purse right there." Or, "I punched her. She snotted off to me, so I punched her one, right in the face. She deserved it, she asked for it." That's their rationale.

But I want to just clear up that there is not "good and evil" on the Map. There is not a duality. *There is a change of character in consciousness.* At 1,000, it inspires the world, either consciously or unconsciously. The energy field created by the Great Avatars uplifts and holds this world this very instant. The energy field of everybody in this room is upholding this world this very instant. That which we are at this moment upholds and lifts the world. You see? Is that grandiosity or a fact? "Is that grandiosity?" (No). All right. Okay. "That is a fact which we just stated: resist" (True). That is a fact. Okay. So, periodically, we do kinesiology just to verify something that the ego may have a doubt about.

I hope to clarify, then, that scale of consciousness, we're not talking about a duality of good and evil. We're talking about gradations of Love. That which we call "evil" is merely totally unloving. I have been researching the level of non-Love. I don't advise people to do that. I'll do it; you don't have to bother. And I'm discovering non-Love; in doing this, I'm finishing a book called now *I* in which we try to trace the evolution of consciousness as it appeared within the created universe and track its evolution over time, and its evolution all the way up the scale of life through all the various lifeforms throughout the eons, and as it manifests up to the very highest possible.

As we do that, we notice that life seems to come up two different tracks. One track sort of reaches its greatest perfection in the age of the dinosaurs, in which the life of the individual is at the price, at the cost of the life of another individual. So, the great reptiles, the great dinosaurs lived by the death of others. So, we see that one energy in the world that lives by the death of others is, therefore, the extreme of narcissism. If we were going to define evil, it is the extreme of selfishness: "I wish to live. Therefore, you'll have to die."

The Nature of Causality

So, the other life is immaterial. At the very bottom of that scale, you might say, we find the venomous, so I'm writing a chapter on the venomous. One bite from the venomous, and you are dead. The Komodo dragon is a living example—sort of atavistic. But the truly venomous are much more basic than that. The box jellyfish has something like 26 fatal enzymes, fatal poisons, 26 fatal venoms. It not only kills you once, but it kills you 26 different times and ways. Wow, is that necessary? I mean, won't one poison do it? The black mamba, who calibrates, I think, around 35, also has all these neurotoxins. However, I find that the ultimate culprit is a little mollusk that lives at the bottom of the sea, who has a long Latin name which I can't remember. He apparently burrows through the shell of his prey and injects a magnificent cocktail of 40 fatal enzymes—40 poisons. One's enough to kill you, and then they did it again, and then they did it again, each one a different enzyme system. That doesn't occur just spontaneously, does it? You just can't say, "Well, by the accidental playing around of evolution, this worked pretty well, so it . . ." No. You begin to see there's an intelligence behind *all* in this universe. The ultimate venom, then, is so potent that it is 40 times what it's needed to be—40 different possible enzymes. We come up through the funnel-web spider, which is also the most vicious creature on the planet. It is also loaded with enough poisons to kill a whole army of people. Why the overdoneness of it? Why the extreme of it?

Anyway, at the same time of the venomous, you see the benign. You see the mammal; you see the domestic animal; the deer isn't killing anybody; it's living off the chlorophyll, the oxygen, the energy of the sun, and it kills nobody. It eats the top off the grass. The grass roots remain. He walks around and he does his elimination, which fertilizes more grass; so, more grass, more rain, more oxygen, more chlorophyll. So, it's like one, the herbivorous, then, supports life. Nobody has to die for a mule to keep on living. Nobody has to die for a cow, a lamb, a sheep. It's as though there's two different lines of evolution going on.

Let's move on now to causality. I'm going to talk about causality, because eventually, spiritual awareness has to do with understanding the nature of creation and the nature of God because they go hand in hand, in a way. And one of the major blocks that keeps people in the 400s and keeps them from evolving is a misunderstanding of the word, the concept of "causality." I think I did speak about it in *Power vs. Force*, but I wanted to go into it a little more differently. There are many ways for spiritual evolution. I'm also working on another book called *Radical Reality: All Stands Revealed [Truth vs. Falsehood],* in which we do like a thousand calibrations of everybody that had any significance that ever lived, and current trends in society; rock music; all the way from Aristotle to current living creatures and places. And it creates an understanding of the nature of consciousness, and how it evolved and expressed itself in mankind over time. In doing that, we also calibrated various spiritual techniques, practices, mantras, teachers, and writings to get an understanding of, how does spiritual knowledge evolve, how does it express itself? How is it utilized by people?

There are very significant spiritual teachers who calibrate in the 200s. Well, the most significant thing we need to know about a spiritual teacher is whether they are over 200. That's all I care about. If they're over 200, they're integrous. If they're under 200, which are some very famous gurus in the world, that are under 200. The most significant thing is that they're over 200. Now, various understandings of how to progress have come along historically, some by religious tradition.

The pathway to Enlightenment, the pathway to the realization of the Presence of God—about which I speak and about which this research is concerned—is the pathway through consciousness itself, the most direct. Probably it's closest to Advaita, closest to Zen, perhaps. On the other hand, it also includes an intensity of devotion. There are ways that take many lifetimes, and the progression is slow—much arduous work and very slow progress. Some mantras make you go weak—it's good to know about that. And some are very good.

We'll just use an example—the difference between "Om" and "A-U-M." Depending on which group you go to, one will say "Om," and another will say "Ah-um," right? Quite a difference. Let's see what the difference is. "Om is over 400" (True); "Om is over 500" (True); "Om is over 600" (True); "Om is 699" (True); "Om is over 700" (True); "Om is over 740" (True); "Om is 780" (True); "Om is 900 (True); "Om is 999" (Not true). "Om" is very high. Let's do "A-U-M." "Aum is over 200" (Not true). Thank you. Some spiritual groups have been doing "Aum" for centuries, and to tell you the truth, they get nowhere.

So, there are very serious spiritual errors in the works of really highly esteemed teachers. That error is written up; I just read it, reviewed it the other day—Patanjali's sutras, yoga sutras, translated by Satchidananda. It's called *Integral Yoga: The Yoga Sutras of Patanjali*. That error is right in that book—so you're a devotee, and you read this; it's by Satchidananda, translation of Patanjali. You say this one has got to be the truth. Don't believe it. Don't believe anything unless you check it out yourself. Or have somebody who understands how to check things out check it out for you. Which is one reason I'm working on the current book, which will give a thousand calibrations, because a lot of people don't have the time and the energy, and they're not really interested in kinesiology. I myself am not really interested in kinesiology any more than Galileo was interested in telescopes. He thought telescopes were very boring, but they revealed a staggeringly interesting universe, which is what kinesiology is to me. It's rather tedious, but it reveals information you can't get any other way.

Certain information is, of itself, just to know it can save many a lifetime of spiritual endeavor. Some things, the information itself, is so staggering that it instantly jumps your consciousness ahead of time.

I forgot something at the start of this. "I have permission: resist" (True). "To go back to the beginning: resist" (True). "The consciousness level of the audience is over 400" (True); "410" (True); "412" (Not true). "The level is over 410" (True); "411" (Not true); 410 to 411—just remember that for later. We usually calibrate the consciousness level of the audience before we give the lecture and then after. If it goes down, *pow*! "They were okay until they got here."

Certain bits of information have a great value. Just to have heard it, to get it, jumps you ahead enormously. So usually, you wait until the students are very advanced, and then you present these concepts. I say, "Heck, let's put them right in the beginning, because the information itself already is transformative." All right.

So, we want to look through the illusion of causality, because causality blocks, creates a perceptual block that you cannot see what is actually going on, and you cannot really experience the Presence of God, in a way. It's a great blockade. The Newtonian paradigm, the world of the ego, the world of the intellect, the way the ego's structured, sees a "this" causing a "that." The whole paradigm of our society is based on "a 'this' causes a 'that.'" The Supreme Court upholds it. Scientists verify it. It's built into the language. The newspaper headlines say it; the movies reveal it. It's all-prevailing in our society. Consequently, becoming enlightened in this world is difficult, because the mind, the ego, feelings—you're barraged continuously, around the clock by a paradigm of reality which is based on duality. There's always a "this" causing a "that." The whole judicial system—"I was standing on a street corner, and there was an accident, and that gave me a heart attack!" Right. The court agrees, gives him a half million dollars. The insurance company pays.

So, this paradigm of causality, the courts have now spread so extreme. If I walk down the sidewalk out there and trip and fall, then I can sue this place here. The sidewalk was crooked, or too rough, or too smooth, or there should have been a warning sign there. If there's a warning sign there and it's lit up, it's only in English, you understand? It's not in foreign languages. I mean, I have testified in front of juries that have agreed. "Caution: wet floor." But it wasn't in Spanish. Oh, okay, there you go. And some fellow gets here from Russia. He says, "It's not in Russian. I'm suing!" So you have to have it in every language on the planet. Then he'd say, "Well, I didn't see it. It wasn't lit up." Oh, it wasn't lit up; we'll have to give him an award. Right? It wasn't lit up; it wasn't in every foreign language. How about the size? "The letters were only this big, and I had trouble seeing it." The letters should be this big, according to the jury. So, you see how bizarre it is.

So, now, causality is a very important roadblock. It's a major roadblock. Practically nobody gets beyond the 400s. In our society, what percent get beyond the 400s? Hmm. "In our society, current society, over one percent of the population gets beyond the 400s." (True.) "Two percent." (Not true.) It is very rare to get beyond the 400s. Even Freud didn't make it, Einstein, Sir Isaac Newton, Bacon, all the great minds. The intellect is the great block. And the reason it is such a great block is that its whole basis is causality. There is always a "this" causing a "that." That's a dualistic perception; that's called dualism—a "this" and a "that." That's why we tried to wipe out duality when it comes to the Map of Consciousness®. There's no "good" and "evil" there. It's all a gradation; there are no opposites.

CHAPTER 2

There Is Only One Variable

What we did in explaining how we're going to prove the Map of Consciousness® is applicable to all seeming dualities. In a duality, there's only one variable, and it goes like this: from intense to less intense. There are not two variables. There are not two variables—good versus evil, hot versus cold. Cold is not the opposite of hot. Hot has no opposite. Heat is either there or not there, but that doesn't make it its opposite. Electricity is either in the wire, or it is not in the wire. Electricity doesn't have an opposite called "no electric." You can't send "no electricity" down the wire. You can only send electricity. This is the whole key. If you just get what I am saying today, it advances your consciousness enormously.

Things are, more or less, one variable. There are not two variables. How much absence of Love must there be before *your* perception would say, "Well, that's evil?" That depends, right? You're always dealing with only an arbitrary perception. So, the world of duality, then, is the product of an arbitrary positionality.

There is no "this" causing a "that." That is all bizarre illusion. There is the unfoldment of the universe as it proceeds thusly. If we look for a cause—let's take cause as far as we can in the logical world. For a speck of dust to be right where it is—there it is, right there. Anyway, that speck of dust—it's all in your head, there's no speck of dust

up there. For this speck of dust, what causes this piece—
this takes something simple, a speck of dust? We're not
talking about the whole industrial complex or the political structure of the United States or something. We're just
talking about one lousy, little piece of dust. For this little piece of dust to be here, what is the cause? Well, the
cause would, you know, depend on the barometric pressure today. It would depend on the movement of the air
in this room, which would depend on the temperature,
which would depend on how many people are here and
the dimensions of the room. It also depends—for a room
to be here, there has to be land; there has to be a state for a
county to be in; there has to be a planet for that to be on.
That planet is not alone in the universe. It has got to be
whirling around with other universes; and for the planet
to be where it is so this state can be where this county is,
where this building is, where these air currents are, and
all these people are, and this speaker here pointing his
finger up in the air—that's all due to the evolution of all
preceding time, is it not? All of the preceding time had
to evolve for all the planets to be where they are, for the
universe to be where it is, so that this state can be this
place on the globe at this point in time, where this barometric pressure and the atmospheric pressure and these
temperatures and gradations and this light coming down
and making little air currents, and the breath from my
speaking voice. There's an infinite number of *finite* causes,
acting in concert throughout all of time. All of time has to
have occurred up to the moment for this little speck.

Anyhow, we want to get rid of causality. The "cause,"
even within the linear domain, of anything, is the totality
of All That Is, throughout all of time. That is the "cause"
of anything.

Causality: The Major Roadblock to Experiencing the Presence of God

The work we do is continuous. We discover things all the time that are mind-boggling. Since we wrote *Power vs. Force*, many things that we said in there have shifted and changed. That means consciousness is evolving. Spiritual research in the past didn't exist. Consciousness research is the only approach that I know to really investigate the reality behind the world's teachings. Some of them, as we demonstrated before—the difference between "Om" and "Aum"—are quite amazingly different. So, many errors are very important to discover. And the reason that Enlightenment is so extremely rare is that, first of all, very few people are motivated. Not too many people have as much karmic momentum by the time they get through a lifetime on this planet. Life is pretty much set against it. The chances of becoming enlightened are very slim, statistically. We were talking before about the structure of the ego and how it prevails in society. But the other thing that prevails, about which I write quite a bit, somewhat, in *The Eye of the I* and more powerfully in the book I'm finishing now called *I,* is, spiritual error has also prevailed immensely. Not only do you have the world of the ego which you have to deal with, which you incorporated as yourself, but religious error prevails.

Many common spiritual sayings are absolutely baloney. People spend their whole lives—their spiritual communities babble these sayings, and they just accept them at face value. They're not only fallacious; they're actually erroneous. They're completely erroneous. "All things are possible to God"—there's one you hear all the time. No, I'll tell you what's not possible to God is "not-Godness."

"Not-Godness" is not possible to God, you know what I'm saying? "All things are possible to God"—I mean, you hear these ridiculous statements.

We're going to go back to causality and try to remove that as a major roadblock, because it blocks the awareness of karma, blocks the awareness of the Presence of God, and the purpose of consciousness work is to discover the Presence of God within. Religion's concerned with the Presence of God without. God is transcendent, elsewhere in time and place. Even Christianity—you lead a good life, you go to heaven, and there's where God is. God is in heaven. Although Jesus did counter that with "Heaven is within you." Thank goodness. He did say that. So, God is both immanent and transcendent.

That which is all-prevailing could hardly just come right up to the periphery of you and stop there. Logic tells you God is everywhere in the universe; then that within you, the Source of life, obviously, is within yourself. How to come to the knowingness of that and the conscious awareness of the Presence of God is the purpose of these lectures and the purpose of the spiritual research, which brings us back, then, to the great block of causality.

Causality constantly reinforces perception, which is dualistic. There's a "this" and a "that." It presumes separation. In the world of duality and the world of the ego, it makes sense that you're "here" and God is "there." Religion, every sermon, every Sunday morning is about the fact that you're here and God's there. So, how are you going to experience the Presence of God, who disappeared after Chapter 1 in Genesis and you're not going to see Him again until heaven if you've been a good girl or boy, you know? Ah, God. So, traditionally the enlightened, the person who comes into enlightenment by virtue of one reason or another, has been called the "mystic." The mystic is one whose experience of God is in the immediate presence as all-prevailing, and the Source of the Self, the Source of one's own life. [It is] the speakingness and the inspiration out of which the voice is talking, because the personal ego died on January 10, 1965. It's never returned.

The speakingness happens of its own; it's not *caused* by anything. There's no *cause* for this speakingness; there's no *cause*, you understand? It is the manifestation of That Which Is as it spreads out. There's no cause to this speakingness here. This speakingness is happening of its own. Understand that? Nothing is causing this speaking to speak— nothing—except the Presence of God. The only source of anything happening is the evolution of the Presence of God as evolving in this moment.

There is no "this" causing a "that." That is an artifact of perception. How does movement and change come about? So, let's talk about what is the nature of God, because it's helpful to know where you're going before you take an arduous trip to get there, understand? Nobody thinks of that.

The Old Testament God is sort of ill and psychotic and bizarre, very arbitrary. I mean, you wouldn't even take Him in your spiritual class—anybody who lived and thought that way: "We're going to get even with them, trash those people out, kill them, and I've got my favorite few and . . ." I mean, you know, this guy wouldn't even make it to guru!

So, in the midst of that, Christ comes with a new message where it was quite unwelcome. Christ was put to death for revealing the truth, as was John the Baptist.

If there's no "this" causing a "that," how does what we witness come about? All right. Let's say that God being all-prevailing and infinitely powerful is like a giant electromagnetic field. Now, the difference between power and force is, force goes from "here" to "there," and in doing that, it expends its energy. Force goes like this and now gets worn out, and it collapses. All empires come to an end; all wars come to an end; all force exhausts itself because force has to be fed energy from elsewhere. It's limited. Force results in counterforce. When I consult with foreign governments, I tell them: "If you exert force, they will come back with counterforce. You'd better make sure you have got more force than they got." I say, "The better way is to support and love the head of the other government, in return for which he will drop his force. He doesn't need it anymore, and now he will be your friend." Headlines said that worked, yeah?

Power stands there, affects all within its radiation, requires no expenditure of energy, does not expend energy; it sustains. It is what it is, and its power radiates forth with no dimensions. Gravity—it just stands there. Gravity doesn't go from "here" to "there." The power of God does not move from "here" to "there." It is a standing field out of which all of life evolves, yeah? How does what appears to be happening occur? See, there are no happenings in the world. A happening is an arbitrary point of view of the ego. You say, "Start," and that's a happening; "Stop," that's a happening between "start" and "stop." You could have said, "Start 'here'" [at another point]; you could have said, "Stop 'there.'" There is no such thing as a happening; this is an illusion of perception. Therefore, you don't have to explain any happenings, because there are none, so that saves you a lot of work.

How do things come about in the universe? In the beginning, there was the Light; and Light shone forth and represents the expression of God as the universe:

continuous, ever present, without beginning and without end. Out of this infinite potentiality, the nature of God is Unmanifest as infinite potentiality. Even within the physical domain, one cubic inch of empty space has more power than is represented by the total weight of the entire universe. That's even within advanced theoretical physics. In the nonlinear domain, even that is miniscule. There is no limit to the power, potential power, in any infinitely small point in space. We'll explain why that is so.

All that exists, exists. The Source of all that exists, then, is the Unmanifest. The Source of all that exists is God, manifesting what seems to exist as creation. It appears sequential because the unfoldment of the universe is perceived by perception as evolving in time, which is just an illusion of the ego. There is no such thing as "time"; nor is there "space." Anyway, what seems to be happening—how does it come about—and this will explain karma and take care of what happens to you after you leave the body, et cetera.

The spirit, then, is like this "you" or your "spirit" or what you want to call yourself—"entity"—is a speck of dust, see? Now, the movement of every speck of dust, then, depends on the power of the field of gravity, which dominates everything within this room. The field of gravity doesn't move, but everything within it, if it's a giant electromagnetic field, moves depending on the charge on the particle and its polarity and its size, and its position among all the other particles.

Karma, then, is the charge on your particle, the spirit within you. The spirit within you, then, by virtue of the various choices and decisions, develops, you might say, analogous to a certain polarity, a certain position within, in relationship to every other particle. So, everything in the universe is absolutely perfectly aligned with where it is because of what it is, because of what it is. Everything merely is what it is, and as a result of being what it is, its fate is sealed.

The heavens, the hells, the purgatories are nothing but the nonphysical extension, because life is continuous. Because of the nonduality of Reality, there is only life. There is no such thing as "not life." And, if you have life now, you cannot become "not life." God cannot become "not God." That which *is* cannot become "non-is-ness." Consequently, that which is a spirit, as it leaves the body, merely gravitates to its own gravitational harmony. That's obvious.

I was in psychoanalysis with an atheistic psychoanalyst. He was a professor of psychiatry and psychoanalysis at Columbia University. He was a prize catch as an analyst. In those days, you were who your analyst was. I had Lionel Ovesey. He was a full professor at Columbia and a training analyst at the Columbia [University Center for] Psychoanalytic [Training and Research]. At the time, I was an atheist, and he was an atheist. We both took a dim view of religion. Nobody had ever heard of out-of-body experience, and we both agreed with Freud that God was a projection from the unconscious, a father figure about which everybody was ambivalent; you feared God and you hated Him at the same time, et cetera.

So in the middle of all this, I got very sick one time, and I was in this hospital bed, and the next thing I know, I was six feet over the bed. I had never heard of an out-of-body experience. Here I am, invisible, no weight, suspended in time and space, you might say—painless; it was wonderful. I looked down and there's Dave lying in the bed; I mean, he was a mess, I tell you. Yeah, he's not long for this world. He looked rather poorly. I could think, hear, feel; and the sense of self, the presence of who am "I," the

"I" was up here. The "I" was definitely not there. Not only that, but—although it sounds alarming to people who have never heard of it—the capacities, the senses exist in the etheric body, not in the physical body. So, although the ears and the eyes and all that were lying in the bed in that body there, I could see and hear and feel, remember, and see and do everything fine. I didn't need that physicality at all. I later went back in it. I forget how I went back in it—sort of a snap, I think. When I told my analyst about that, we both agreed that it was probably due to the infection—a toxic psychosis of some kind, in which we had created a dual physicality and projected it somehow. Anyway, we were both happy with that. I never told anybody about it in any way, the same as the near-death experience that I'd had early in life. I'd never told anybody about that at all. I never did, until 1995. Such things were not heard of.

By the way, on the TV, they are always confusing *near-death* and *out-of-body*. They think they're the same thing; they're so naive. They're two totally different things. If you calibrate the level of an out-of-body experience, you're pretty much the same person that you were before. Smarter—you know that you're not just a physical body, so there is a spiritual advance. But, a near-death experience, you see a transformation. There is a huge leap in level of consciousness. So anyway, they're not the same thing at all.

So, the nature of God, then, is the infinite power of such an immense degree. In '65 and then again—the consciousness kept advancing over the years—there would be a new condition in which the power of God became even more revealed—staggering, staggering. This power is absolute. There is nothing that can oppose the power of God. There is no opposite to the power of God. Nothing is

possible, any more than "non-God-ness" is possible. That
which is "All That Is" is infinite power. When I first saw
that power, I was just [shocked beyond measure]; the mind
disappeared; all thoughts stopped, and the body moved
of its own, which it does to this day. It's always doing sur-
prising—look what it's doing now—I mean, it just does all
kinds of things. It does it all by itself, see. People say, "Why
do 'you' do that?" See the duality? There's a "me" and then
a "body." It just does what it does by its lonesome. I mean,
it's amusing and it's a lot of fun, but it's got nothing to do
at all with who I am. I so often look at it and I can't believe
it's even there. However, it took many years to get used
to running it. It's like running things by remote control.
The "you" is over there, and everybody is talking to the
"you," and you wonder who they're talking to. There isn't
any "me" there at all, you know. They're talking to that
physicality.

▲ ▲ ▲

We're going to get back to causality. So, here is everything within the universe being what it is. That's all it
can do. There's no "this" that does a "that." Everything
is every instant, the perfect expression of that which it is
at this instant. As a consequence, it's being what it is at
this instant ("instant" being a point of perception, and
no such thing as an "instant" actually existing), but at
this particular instant its polarity, its choices, its wisdom,
its life experiences are held within this enormous gravitational field. You see how it's automatic. You see why the
justice of God is absolute. The idea of an arbitrary God
who judges you at death is idiotic beyond belief. That
which you are automatically goes to that which it is. It

has no choice in the matter, does it? That which you are automatically gravitates to that which it is.

You can take an old bar and grill. A new buyer buys it, cleans it up, and puts drapes, curtains, new carpets; it's all glossed up. Does the old crew come back to the bar and grill and say, "Gee, Henry, this place looks great now"? No, they don't go there anymore. It doesn't appeal to them at all. A waterfront dive is a waterfront dive. You clean it up, put new drapes and all—it stinks. Who the hell wants to go there? Nobody wants to go there. You get drunk and throw up on the floor, and they get all excited about that; you know what I mean? Who wants to hang out there? You get in a brawl, and they call the cops. Who wants to hang out in a joint like that? Where does a guy from a waterfront dive go when they clean up his old hangout? He goes to another waterfront dive, that's where he goes. He's attracted to that which he is, you understand? He's not attracted if I say, "Here's a free ticket that'll take you to see the Pietà." He'll say, "Can I sell it? How much is it worth?" So, one automatically gravitates to that which one is, you might say. You are that which you already are.

Some people are attracted to beauty, the great cathedrals of Europe. When I traveled to Europe, I went from one cathedral to another. The attraction was to experience Chartres, the blue window in Chartres, and Westminster Abbey. The things that inspire and attract you, then, reflect that which you are. So, even before I became that which I am, I was already that which I am, but seemed to be that which I was at the time, which is already attracted to what I really was, which was the great cathedrals. Anyway, I calibrated the great cathedrals; they are 700, 700. Westminster Abbey, the great cathedrals, Notre Dame, they're stunning. Great beauty always makes you cry. I avoid it because I become totally incapacitated—just the memory of those cathedrals; the sacrifice of all the people over hundreds of years, spending a whole lifetime just to carve one pulpit—I mean, just the enormity of the devotion, which is the second way to God, which I don't talk about because it cannot be talked about. The pathway to God I speak about is probably most closely aligned, as I said, with Zen or Advaita. It's rather radical reality, radical truth, and you can talk about it. The way through the heart cannot be talked about!

As you remove the barriers, the way through the heart becomes more powerful. The classic yogas are through the mind and through the heart. The great cathedral brings forth enormous, overwhelming experience of Divine Love and the presence of Divine Love as the Self—and that incapacitates you. So, I try to stay away from Love, because that brings everything to a halt.

So, everything is merely being what it is as a result of the nature of Creation itself, whose capacity is infinite, whose Presence is always present, and who sustains your life. The evidence of the Presence of God within you is your existence. That one exists is the demonstration and the proof of the existence of God. That which the ordinary mind takes for granted is the very Source of the awareness of the presence of Divinity as existence.

What is the source of existence if it is not causality? If one's existence is not the end of a bunch of old billiard balls going through time and coming out as one labeled "you," then how does one come into manifestation, huh? The only source of existence, the capacity for existence, is Divinity. Nothing in the universe has the power to create existence, nothing.

Causality is the thinnest of flimsy attempts to rationalize how it could otherwise come about by that which does not wish to acknowledge its source as God, which is how you get to the lower astral dimension. The lower astral is the place for those who deny God. It's a different dimension than this. It's a different dimension.

There is an infinite number of dimensions, each one evolving in infinite directions. This [dimension] is only one [of them]. How can it be infinite and ever expanding and never stopping? Because the energy of Creation, the Presence of God—one innate quality of the Presence of God is Creation; therefore, that which is created has within it the energy of God which continues to create; and that which is created continues to create. Therefore, out of one dimension evolves an infinite number of dimensions. Out of each of the infinite number of dimensions evolves an infinite number of dimensions—do you understand—the expansive universe?

The awareness that the Self is the source of an infinite series, of an infinite series, of an infinite series of dimensions calibrates over what? "Calibrates over 1,000" (True); "1,100" (True); "1,200" (True); "1,250" (True); "1,280" (True); "1,290" (Not true). That which is the source of one's Self is also the Source of all the dimensions; you're not limited to just this dimension. You are only expressing yourself as this dimension. That's just a recent discovery.

To understand, then, your relationship to God and karma—karma is merely what one has become throughout the various lifetimes. At 600, you see there's only one lifetime. You see that—they are not an infinite number, but quite a few incarnations. It's just a recall of one life. It's *this* life one remembers—being a pickpocket in Paris and various things like that. It's only just within memory; it's just who you are, or had been, and what was learned there.

Therefore, what you've become automatically goes as a continuum. It's just one life you have. There's only one life. There are not multiple lives. There's no such thing as going from life to non-life, and then back to life, and then incarnating, and all. There's only one life, and so long as you identify with the body, you limit the memory to this body's life. As you no longer identify "me" or the self as this physicality, then the memory of all the other lifetimes comes back. Many people have memories of previous lifetimes when they go out of the body. Once they escape this body, they can see all the lives.

So, karma, then, is merely the accumulated energy. So, every action affects your calibrated level of consciousness. So the spirit body, which has a classic name, is sort of like a little computer. It keeps track of where you are in time and space and all your merits, demerits, et cetera.

So, that brings us to a recalibration. This is a great moment in time. We are going to change these calibrated levels of consciousness. You don't want somebody in the 700s as president of the United States. It just won't work. They wouldn't have any interest at all. We found that great leaders of great religions should be around 570. You cannot run a huge organization, like the Catholic Church, over 600. It wouldn't make any sense at all. And you don't have enough power, spiritual power, in the 400s. At 570, we have Pope John Paul II. 570 is Unconditional Love—he tries to bring everybody together and heal up the past as best he can. The Dalai Lama runs around 570. If you're going to be the great leader of a great world church, you ought to be around the ideal of 570. If you want to be the president of the United States, you'd better be around 450.

All the great presidents are really around 450. The signers of the Constitution and the Declaration of Independence were more in the 500s. And the Constitution of the United States calibrates at 700, higher than any country I know of. But, to be a president, you'd better be smart and around 450. 450 is the intellect, the capacity to really handle this world. If you're going to be a great political leader, you'd better be around 450, or you're going to get your socks beat off.

At 500 and up, one isn't interested in that anymore. Worldly power is uninteresting, and politics are only interesting to the degree that they reflect a certain spiritual truth. What I wanted to do is to say is that one is not better than the other. And many of my favorite people are in the 300s. They're very willing. 310 is Willingness. "Yeah, let me do it, let me help; let me . . ." They're great people to be with; they'd build the whole world. The whole world is built by people in the 300s. We have a crew working for us that has a little white dog. This little white dog, whom I never met before—here's this workman, he's a one-dog contractor. You know, they come with one dog, two dogs, et cetera. This little dog goes everywhere with him, loyal as can be. So, here's this white dog, whom I'd never met before and he'd never met me, and this dog comes right over, just instantly loving you—instantly loving you; just glad to see you and, "Gosh, let's be friends." And boy, instantly, we are like intimate loving pals. Instant Love, huh? We calibrated that dog. Let's do that dog. That dog, who is up in the audience right now. "That dog, we have permission, right?" (True); "He's 500" (True); "He's over 5" (True); "501" (True); "502" (True); "504" (True); "505" (True); "506" (True); "507" (True); "508" (Not true). He's about 505 to 508.

Pure Love, huh. The first time I calibrated a dog's wagging tail and got 500, I said, "Whoa, half the people on the planet don't." We calibrated our cat's purr. Let's get Kitty's purr. Oh, I *love* that kitty. Kitty's purr is over 500: resist" (True); "502" (True); "504" (True); "505" (Not true). Kitty's purr. Kitty just sits there, just radiating pure Love. So, here, Love comes through the animal kingdom without intellect. People look down on the animal because it doesn't have intellect. See, that's the ego. They say, "The animals don't have an ego." Can't get screwed up like humans. This dog just comes over and loves you, like that! Isn't that great? No wonder people love their animals. People say, "Why, he's sick. He thinks more about his dog than he does other people." Well, the people around him calibrate about 190, and his dog calibrates at 500.

Isn't that strange, huh? That Love comes up then—it is like two channels. One is a channel of that which is venomous, poisonous, hatred, and it brings about death. Then there's that which is nurturing, benign, peaceful, and serves as an avenue for Love. In my view, Love manifested within the physical domain by motherhood. There was no Love—the dinosaur doesn't love its eggs. It just lays an egg and goes off, right? There's the maternal, the mother who cares about the child. That's when Love began to shine on the earth. There was no Love in the world of dinosaurs. Show me some Love in the world of dinosaurs—it doesn't exist there. Everything eats everything else.

Levels of Consciousness Are Different, Not Better

I just got off on that tangent because I didn't want people to think that "this" is better than "that." Somebody at 700 is not suitable as a carpenter, is not suitable to run a church, is not suitable as a president. You don't want anybody at 700; most of them can't function at all. They just sit in their ashram, and if they still survive, people come and say hello to them, and they smile happily at them, and that's that. You don't want people down at the bottom, either. There's one restaurant [where] I used to eat breakfast, and I stopped going there because of the low calibration of the waitress. The calibration of the waitress was so bad, I couldn't handle it. I would go there all the time in Prescott, and every time I'd go there, she'd say, "Do you want a menu?" Like she never saw me before. "You want a menu?" Sort of confrontational. "You want coffee?" I'd ordered tea the last 20 times. I'm the only customer in the restaurant at that time—there's nobody else. Every Tuesday morning for months, I'd ordered the same thing. "You want coffee?" No! She never stops talking. She's opinionated about everything. I can't stand the energy of this place. It was convenient, that's all. All right. She calibrates—I don't want to calibrate her.

Then there's another restaurant I go to, and they say, "Oh, hi, I haven't seen you all week. You want tea? You want your usual?" That's where I eat every morning—Monday, Wednesday, and Friday morning. They know what you want. *Of course* they recognize you; you've been there every freaking morning, you know what I'm saying?

When we wrote the book *Power vs. Force*, 85 percent of the world's population calibrated below 200. That leaves us 15 percent here in the 200s, who are the builders of the world, the construction workers, the steelworkers, the people who go to work every day. They're the backbone of our society, and the 200s and the 300s. The 400s is the world of the intellect and reason that dominates America; 500 is rare; 540 is extremely rare, and from 540 and up, there's practically nobody. The thing is that their power is so enormous that they counterbalance the rest of the whole population.

That which is over 200 is integrity. So, integrity means honesty, the honesty of one's convictions, and, if in truth, you cannot find God through the intellect, which is what I tried to do—you cannot find God through the intellect. And you have to really warp logic a little bit to get there.

And, going through God as "first cause": if you go back through this—as we were talking about "causality"—you'd say, well, "God is 'first cause.'" No, that can't be, because the sequence is not of "sameness." You suddenly come to "differentness." The quality of God is not the same as the quality of the supposed effect, so you cannot find the original billiard ball behind all the billiard balls. Because when you get past number one, there are no billiard balls there. You will not find another billiard ball behind billiard ball number one. If you can see through that conundrum, that's like a koan, and you'll become enlightened.

All right. So, there's no "cause" for what happens, but there is a source. The source is the structure of the ego itself as it sits within the infinite power of spiritual consciousness, and that automatically sequences—what appears to be sequence—the fate of the spirit. And that is the absolute perfection of the judgment of God. There is no error possible. Therefore, there is no "God" to fear; there's only the consequences of one's own actions to fear, which then gets projected onto a God figure, which has no reality and no existence.

So, to see through the illusion of causality, there's nothing causing anything out there. Nothing is causing anything else. What you see are conditions. For this flower to open up, it requires a certain temperature, a certain humidity, a certain amount of sunlight, nurturance—and as you see it opening up, the sunlight is not causing it to open, the nurturance is not causing it to open; nothing is causing it to open, because everything fulfills its own potential. So, within that which is created, that which comes into existence, part and parcel of its existence is its innate capacity to manifest as that which it is. The becoming of that which is witnessed as existence, then, is merely the unfolding of the potentiality of that as it was created. It's not being caused by anything over here; it's not being caused by anything over there. Is that clear?

There Are Different Dimensions

In New Age communities, channeling is very popular. Certain prophets—Biblical prophets, scriptures—also were really channelers; they were channeling another entity on the other side. All right. Channeling is, then, a capacity to communicate with spiritual energies that are not within the physical domain. They are based, however, within duality. There's a "this" and a "that." There's a "me," the channeler, and there's a "that," the spirit. There's a duality there which already sets a limit on the degree of erudition that can come through that way. So if a person is going to dabble in channeling—I don't recommend channeling— but if a person is going to dabble in channeling, always get the calibration level of the entity on the other side and the entity on this side, because the lower astral is a great source of channeling and psychics.

In a channeling, there is a "this" and a "that." There's a "me" and a "you." There's an entity "there" and a "something" here. That's different than the way to enlightenment, because enlightenment is merely the progressive awareness of the Source of one's existence, which is neither here nor there and has no positionalities. It has no personalities; it has no "either/or–ness." See, you're either

the channeler or the source, et cetera. There's no "either/
or–ness" because that which prevails within all is identical
within all. I can't explain it other than that.

All those sorts of New Age things, always calibrate
the level of truth first before you get involved with them,
because a lot of them are quite intriguing. The lower astral,
that denies God, is in competition with that which affirms
God and is in competition for dominion of this planet.
That's a thesis I'm working out in the book *I*. There's competition. As you remember in *Power vs. Force*, the level of
consciousness of mankind was at 190 for many, many centuries. Mankind never got over—beginning with Neanderthal man, who calibrates around 70; Cro-Magnon man
also calibrates only about 70. It's only very recently that
Homo sapiens even appeared, and *Homo sapiens* was also
dominated by the lower astral realm. And it was only in
the late '80s that the consciousness level of mankind went
over 200. It's as though the lower astral held dominion
over this globe, and the spiritual energy came in, and
another life came up through the lambs and the herbivorous and reached full manifestation through maternal
love. And it's as though the lower astral held dominion
over this plane—this planet—until the late '80s. The consciousness level then went over 200. The lower astral was
no longer in total control.

The Difference between Enlightenment
and Salvation

What is the difference between enlightenment and salvation? That's a very astute question. I myself went through
a conflict: would Jesus be my main guru, or the Buddha?
It seemed like Jesus stood for salvation, and the Buddha

stood for enlightenment. Are they two different things? Yes, they are, in a way. Jesus Christ taught salvation. Although He taught that the Presence of God is within you, the mystic, usually through the pathway of the heart, discovered that God, being Love, is innate within you. But generally, what Jesus sort of agrees with is Lotus Land Buddhism. The Buddha of infinite compassion—those of you who are Buddhists know the name of it: Avalokiteśvara. There's all these different representations of Buddha, different names. Anyway, Pure Land Buddhism is very much like Christianity. It's assumed that the negativity of this world is so severe that the chances of reaching enlightenment are practically zero. It is not, therefore, a practical goal. If you realize that the consciousness level of mankind was at 190 until the late 1980s, it means that you're trying to reach the highest state from a severely negative gravity field, you might say. It was not practical.

And certainly, when you look at the population in which Jesus taught—illiterate, nomadic, believing in gods that were sort of demonic—if you calibrate the gods of the Old Testament, they come out about 70 or 90: vengeful, angry, vain, egotistical, narcissistic; primitive gods, the same as the gods of ancient Rome and other primitive societies, sort of demonic. "Projections of the unconscious"—that's the God that Freud said had no reality. The gods of the Old Testament are projections from the unconscious, Freud said. And then he made a mistake; he said, "Therefore, God doesn't exist," when he should have said the negative gods are invalid. He didn't—he went beyond. He said, "Therefore, God doesn't exist." Carl Jung, who calibrates at 520, Jung went beyond that. He didn't say that "because the false gods are false, therefore a true God doesn't exist." On the other hand, Carl Jung affirmed the validity of the spirit, the spirit world; so Jung crossed over from 499, crossed that great barrier at 500.

The purpose of Christ, then, is the same as Lotus Land Buddhism: that without Divine help, the likelihood of getting to heaven is slim. One needs the powerful energy, the Great Avatar, at 1,000. To merely affirm that that is your teacher will carry you through. And we asked this question ourselves. The Buddha teaches the way to enlightenment. Jesus Christ teaches the way to salvation. Let's see if that's correct. "That is correct: resist" (True). That is correct. Now let's see who needs salvation. "Entities over 600 need a savior: resist" (Not true). "Entities over 540 need a savior: resist" (True). All right, so less than 600, one needs a savior. Okay, let's see. All right. Is there another question on this subject? Jesus Christ teaches the way of salvation. It is even taught within certain schools of Buddhism and the Hindu that the way which I tend to teach, the way through consciousness itself, is not suitable because of the extent of the negativity of the world. The one-pointedness of mind—we'll get into that; how in a meditative state, to absolutely transcend the ego, it happens in a snap. Suddenly, one is the Source out of which all that—it's obvious—that one is the Source out of which all of that manifests, but it's not obvious until it happens.

The Buddha then taught a way which is suitable for the minority. The Buddha said: "Once you hear of enlightenment, you will eventually reach it because the spirit will now choose spiritual pathways, lifetime after lifetime." The Buddha did not say that by arduous spiritual commitment, you're likely to get enlightened in this time, although it did happen as such. The Buddha represents more what I write about, then—the realization of the Self as the Source of all existence. One comes into that awareness at 600, as the presence of an infinite Love. In the 700s, which is the level of the sage, one realizes the Self as Divinity. And that there is nothing but the Self, and the rest is perceptual impressions projected by the mind.

So, it is wise to have a Savior. And it is wise even if you're beyond 600, to value the great gift and the Divinity of the Savior. To realize the absolute truth of that which you are, there is nothing to save. There's nothing that needs salvation.

Enlightenment and Salvation

Enlightenment and salvation—is that sufficient? Is salvation necessary? And if so, what are you being saved from? Now, salvation, then, has to do with the level one reaches as you leave the body. You see, Jesus says, "Those who hold me in mind, to whom I am now bound by your commitment to me, I will provide the energy you need to reach the heavenly realm." Lotus Land and Christianity are both very practical. Both also were a teaching in a time of great ignorance. Don't forget, the Buddha was born in 500 B.C. There was no printing press; nobody was educated; nobody could read or write. The level of awareness was almost a primitive level of the basics of life and nothing beyond that. So, Lotus Land Buddhism, then, is also the same teaching that you, of your own, are not likely going to reach enlightenment in this lifetime, because the negativity of life here is so severe. And the commitment is so peculiar, and particular, that one in 10 million would actually even do that. We'll go into what techniques are involved to transcend the ego, and you will see that it's not going to appeal to too many people. Not to mention, the burning wires are going through your body, and—good

God! But I'll give you just a taste of it. So, the Buddha is the way for one who achieves spiritual merit by following the teachers, like the Buddha. So, the Buddha doesn't say necessarily you will reach enlightenment by following the Eightfold Path this instant, but he's saying that that commitment will automatically guarantee that each lifetime you are on, so once you choose the direction of the Light, the end is certain. And I believe that, that what the Buddha said—is why the phenomenon happened within this lifetime.

Allness vs. Nothingness

In that lifetime, I was a Hinayana Buddhist. I'll tell you that. That's another story. In a previous lifetime, I was a Hinayana Buddhist, and a very devout one too. There are two types of Buddhism, in general: Mahayana and Hinayana. Anyway, my belief system—and I meditated for many years—was that the ultimate truth was Void. The Void is a very tricky concept. As I told you before, there is no opposite to God. There is no such thing as nothingness. But there is a variety of Buddhism which really confuses Void with nothingness, as though there is an opposite to Allness. That's a duality you don't have to transcend until you get up into the 900s, right? "The infinite Reality as Allness versus Nothingness comes up over 900" (True); "910" (Not true). About 900. By 900, you discern, once you pass that. All right. Many of those schools of Buddhism were below 900, so they confuse nothingness and Void. I was very intensely devout and devoted in those lifetimes, and the ultimate reality was Void. When I went out of the body, I went into the Void. There were a number of lifetimes where there was no connection between the lifetimes. There was awareness—blank awareness. That happened right before this lifetime. The awareness of existence came out of nothingness. From nothingness—existence. Well, then it all solved itself. Each time I went out of body in that form of Buddhism where the ultimate Reality was Void, I experienced that which my own mind created: that the ultimate Reality is Void. There is no such thing as an ultimate Reality of Void. But after many lifetimes with powerful meditations upon that truth, I created Voidness as, and today there are mistranslations of the teachings of the Buddha—not mistranslations—but it's not explained in a way that would help you to avoid this error. My own profound belief about the ultimate Reality and my devotion to Buddha was such that I went into nothingness every time I went out of body. However, because that's not a reality, you can't stay in Void, nothingness as Void. You can't stay there, because it's not a reality. Consequently, you find yourself back in another body—bang! It was a sudden explosion when I hit back into this body. This little wagon and this body, called "me" in those days, age three or four, sitting in this wagon, and—*wham*! Suddenly, a sudden confrontation with existence was like, *bang*! Out of nothingness—existence. It was a terrific contrast.

So, the ultimate Reality is not nothingness, but Allness. The totality, the complete, all-inclusive Allness, which is "no thing." It is no-thing. It is not Void; it's All.

The Buddha didn't speak about God, because everybody has belief systems about God, and your belief system will create what you believe God to be, and you'll be pursuing a projection of your own imagination and ignorance. So the Buddha didn't speak of God. He said just forget about that and find the Source of your own consciousness. That is the "Buddha nature." Well, unfortunately, he called it "Buddha nature." Uh-oh. That was a mistake too, so he called it "Void." That's "nothing," right? Now people believe that "nothingness" is a reality, and if you really pursue and become an adept, you're going to experience "nothingness" as the ultimate. It's very powerful. I resolved that conflict one time.

I was in the conflict between Jesus and Buddha, the way of the heart. I had a teacher who had fallen from a higher level. This is something else, which is a thing we'll have to talk about. There are teachers who, when they were teaching, they calibrated in the high 500s; but you calibrate them now, they're in the 200s. There are quite a few of them, and they are all very famous. So there was a conflict. I had a teacher who had at one time been in a very high state; I had not realized he was not in a high state anymore. Anyway, he took all the attributes of God, such as Love, beauty, et cetera, and said those were all attachments, and you should release on those attachments. Okay. Those are all the attributes of God, right? Anyway, that came out of that same Buddhist tradition. Love and the attachment to Love are two different things. I didn't realize that. Anyway, at the time, I said, "Yes, Love is an attachment." He was telling me to let go of beauty, Love, and all that stuff. He was looking down on it as an attachment. I was in conflict between Jesus and Buddha. So, I had the misunderstanding of Buddha as representing the ultimate Reality as Void. And looking at Jesus as Love as an attachment. I was in quite a conflict about it.

Finally, I said no, Buddha's higher than Jesus. Love is an attachment. I started releasing on Love. I went into the infinite Void. Huh. This time, not unconsciously—consciously—went into the Void. Now, I tell you, the Void is very, very impressive. It is *very* impressive. It is a dimension that is beyond some puny little ego; I tell you—the absolute experience of nothingness. Infinite nothingness. There was one thought left. In it, all reality is revealed. You see everything moving of its own nature within the infinite field of the Infinite Reality. So, it does reveal Reality, *starkly*. But there was something wrong. Some innate spiritual intuition, of its own, realized there was an error. It didn't speak; it was just a knowingness. And to let go of that one thought would be like a spaceship takes you out into infinite, unmapped space, lets you out, destroys all maps of where they were, and returns to its base. There is no record of even your existence, much less where; there's no way to return. So, it took enormous energy, enormous power, all the power I could summon, to reinforce that thought and come back out of the infinite space of the Void. At that time, it was a conscious experience. A less sophisticated or less lucky person would be convinced that that is the ultimate reality and let go of the last thought and become as nothingness, which is a paradox in itself, because there is nothing that can become nothingness. But, that experience of nothingness, you could probably hang out there for quite a few eons before you'd discover the error.

So, what was the intuitive knowingness coming out of? It was the intuitive knowingness that the infinite Reality is the quintessence of Love; that it was the absence of Love in that space that was the warning that signaled that it was not *the* perfect space. It was not the ultimate Reality. As a paperboy, when I'd almost frozen to death and I went into a Divine space—and the most profound thing of it, beyond all time, beyond all—you realize that you always existed: before all universes, I am; and after all universes have gone, I will still prevail, that's for sure. Universes are just nothing. You know that in that space, but the most profound thing is like an enormous Love of such a quality that there is no ever mistaking it for anything else again. And the vibration at that level was absent in that infinite Void. So, that sort of answers the difference between salvation and enlightenment. The infinite Reality as Allness, rather than Voidness.

The Void means void of all form. Void of all form, because that which you "Are" is void of all form—that is correct. So, there's a couple of little misunderstandings of Buddhism that are important to understand. The ultimate Void means void of dimension. It means it's nondualistic. Because it is no *thing*; that's why it is All—All. To be All, you can be no thing, nothing, *no thing*: void of all form, void of all qualities, void of all conditions, void of all descriptions. That's why it's all that is. To be everywhere, you cannot be any particular place, because if you are in a particular place, you can't be everywhere. That's my understanding of it. We'll ask the Buddha if that's right! "That explanation is correct: resist" (True).

So, how does one move up the scale? You do it by choice, by commitment, by attraction. It's really a matter of you choose the light rather than the darkness; that's all it is. Choose light over darkness. You choose light over darkness, and if you choose light over darkness, you can still make great mistakes. I remember a mistake. You can make great mistakes, see, because the calibrated level is intention.

CHAPTER 3

The Pathway of Radical Subjectivity

Another question I often get is, "What is radical subjectivity?" It's really the core of that which I teach, or research, or whatever you want to say, to convey to people. The Presence of God reaches awareness by virtue of the fact that you are aware that you are. The difficulty with religion is, it leads you elsewhere. The pathway, in fact, we might even call it the "pathway of radical subjectivity." The Presence of God is knowable as obvious via radical subjectivity. In other words, consciousness devoid of content is only aware that it's aware. All truth is subjective. There is no such thing as "objective" truth. The radical materialist says, "Unless it can be measured and weighed or defined, it's not real." That's scientific materialism—sort of, unfortunately, the direction that psychiatry is going.

The most radical materialist can only say that only the material is real because, subjectively, that seems so. Do you understand? In the end, you always end up back with subjectivity. Who concludes that? And what is it about you that is concluding that? Instantly he's thrown back into the fact that every statement is purely subjective. You can weigh all the evidence, but there has to be something there that agrees and says yes or no. So, the inner condition that is necessary before anything can be said or known—even your own existence—is radical subjectivity. The knowingness, all that is here that you call yourself,

55

is your presence. Your physicality happens to be the baggage in this domain, but what makes you here is your presence. Let's say you go to visit a friend, and you come back again, and your wife says, "Well, did you see George?" "No, he was asleep." If he's asleep, you didn't see George, even though his body's lying there. You didn't meet with George. Why? Because he's not present. Well, if his body was who he was, you'd say, "Yeah, I saw George." "No, he was taking a nap." The presence that we appreciate in each other is the presence of your consciousness.

So, the difference between the two waitresses is, the one waitress is mechanical. The lady who always asked me, "Are you going to have coffee"; she calibrates: "Over 200: resist" (True); "201: resist" (Not true). Yes, she's right at 200. She never looks you in the eye. You know, "Are you going to have coffee?" No, I haven't had coffee the last 20 times I was in here! She never looks at you. That which is unloving has a very hard time being open and looking at you and revealing to you who they are. When you look at them, they quickly look away. They cannot sustain a gaze, a direct gaze; it's frightening.

The subjectivity, then, is the "presence" of that which you are. The one who comes and says, "Oh, hey, I haven't seen you all week, you going to have your usual?" She's very "present," you understand what I'm saying? She's present. The other person is not present. It's hiding behind the physicality of life and the bare-bones form of life, but that person, out of fear, or lack of evolution of consciousness, probably, just isn't that much "there."

Radical truth, then, is a purely subjective state. There is no "this" that experiences a "that." The only difficulty I have with Hinduism is the concept of union: yoga, as "union" of self with God. You see, a self with God. Right away, you've got two, right? There's "you," and there's "God." No, to realize that the Self, with a capital *S*, is the expression of God as your existence, that is enlightenment. The Source and the manifestation of that Source are one and the same thing, you understand?

The way to reach enlightenment is very simple. First of all, one chooses it. One tries to find a teacher that calibrates at a level that you can resonate with. Just because a teacher calibrates very high doesn't mean you're necessarily going to resonate with him. Your best teacher may be somebody who's just a great pal and makes you change your mind, that you're not going to do any more mugging. He's a great teacher. There was a famous teacher of *A Course in Miracles* who used to be a mugger. He died some years ago. He was a mugger on the streets of New York City. He'd say, "We'd stand on the street corner, and we just knew who was 'muggable.' We just knew this one was easy." He then later sort of converted and became a teacher of *A Course in Miracles*.

Anyway, we're all interested in spirituality as a subject, as a direction to go. So, most people are reasonably intelligent who choose this kind of a pathway, and they may check it out. Some people go directly into a religion and just follow that religion sort of rotely. Other people, there's a certain period of searching, a sort of turning around and looking for greater meaning in life; or they may read something that inspires them, and for karmic reasons unknown. Or there may be a period of life. Your life may be very unspiritual and then suddenly, *wham!* You're suddenly interested—it's as though that cycle of life has come up now, and now this priority is coming up. You find a teacher to whom you can relate. He needs to make sense. It has to be a person that you can relate to. Then the next thing would be to check that person out with kinesiology or get somebody that knows how to do it. A thing like kinesiology is boring, but there's a lot of people who do it. Or I'm going to try to list everyone I can think of in this next book I'm going to come out with.

You can just look him up in the "stand on your head and breathe through your nose" group, because there are all kinds of strange teachings. Some of them are so out-landish, I don't know how anybody could assume there's any truth to them, but they do. So, the fact that it is in a spiritual library or spiritual bookstore doesn't mean any-thing, and I've said many a time—everybody's heard me say it—you can go through your spiritual bookstore at home: all the books that make you go weak, throw them in one pile, and all the books that make you strong, throw them in another pile, and you will see right away what is sort of astral diversion and that which is truth. All the books about the end times coming and all, you find they'll end up on this pile over here. A lot of channelings by "Baba this" and "Baba that." The word "Baba," for some reason, itself is not so great. "The term 'Baba' calibrates over 200: resist" (True). "The term 'Baba' as used in modern America is over 200: resist" (True); "202" (Not true). Baba's not such a great title. So, you try to find somebody to whom you can resonate; it makes sense. If there's a teacher around, great—find one who calibrates reasonably high.

See, enlightenment is different than salvation. It doesn't have anything to do with good personhood. It has nothing to do with good personhood. It has to do with a drive to realize the truth. The teachings of the Buddha are, of course, the traditional. The ancient Vedas have profound truth. You try to find something that there's enough information so as to be comprehensible. There are a number of teachers in the 700s who I respect and refer to. Their teachings are cryptic. There's no explanation so that you can't make it work for you. You just start to feel bad that you haven't reached the level where you can understand what that means, but there isn't sufficient meat to the bones. So, some teachings, to me, are just too barebones. So, anyway, you want to calibrate the level of the teacher or the writing, or the book, the mantra, whatever way you're following. The direct path—the direct path—is through consciousness itself.

There is a teacher I hold in high esteem in Korea. If you ask her, "What school do you represent?" She says, "None." I said, "What do you do?" She said, "We just meditate." So her way, then, is to discover the truth through consciousness itself, which is what I wrote about in *The Eye of the I.*

When you sit down to meditate, you notice that the mind is constantly racing and running around. A lot of the teachings try to teach you how to control it. You can't control it. You don't have any control over the mind. The mind exists of its own nature, and it just runs about and does its own thing, just like the body does. There's no point to try to control it. What you do is, you observe what it is that's witnessing and aware of the thoughts is. The first thing to do is to realize, "I am not the body." The next thing to realize is, "I am not the thoughts." You know you're not the thoughts, and you know you're not the mind, because if you told the mind, "Stop thinking," if you were the mind, it would stop. Try telling your mind, "Stop thinking." It couldn't care less what you said. It goes right on thinking. Now, if you were the mind, it would just obey you, and it would stop thinking. The fact that it doesn't stop thinking is because you are not the mind. The mind belongs to the world like the body does. You can tell the body to go without oxygen, but it won't last too long. The body is a manifestation of the world, and so is the mind. Its content is programmed by society, and you don't have any control over that either.

There is a substrate. What is it that God programmed there? So, the innate nature of the mind is the hardware. The thoughts are the software. What happens is, the innocent mind comes in: consciousness with no content. However, it has proclivities which are karmic; proclivities, but no specific content. Then society starts to program it, and so the software begins to pour in. So, when you start to meditate, what's happening is sort of that your hardware is looking at your software. The innate innocence, the capacity for awareness without any content, is still existent within you. The only reason you realize that the mind is thinking is because the thinkingness is happening against a background of non-thinkingness. The only reason you can hear sound is because sound occurs against a background of silence.

There's a lot of noise, you can't hear what's being said. It's only because the somethingness is only apparent, superimposed, within a field of nothingness of no sound. The same with form: because of the emptiness of space, you can witness form. If this room were full of cardboard boxes, we couldn't even see each other. Right? It's because of the absence, because of the void, that the form stands out. So it's against the background of silence that I hear. It's against the emptiness of space that I can witness, right? Similar with the mind—it's only because the screen upon which the mind is playing is blank that you can know what the mind is thinking, correct?

It's the absence of form that allows you to witness this word, then this word, or this picture, this memory. So the field, then, is blank. The only reason you can see what's up there is because that's a blank screen, right? If that was full up, if it was a Jackson Pollock picture, you wouldn't know what's being said. Let's all be a Jackson Pollock picture.

We just read a nice article on Jackson Pollock; it has to do with chaos theory. The drippings on the canvas really can be traced through chaos theory. There's a pattern you see—you know, chaos theory is that behind what appears to be chance, there's actually an organizing field. So that the content of consciousness, then, the content itself tends to come in, through these few levels of consciousness, against the invisible background of the absence of form, appears form in the form of thought. All right, so the first thing to observe is that the only way you know what the mind is thinking is by observation. So instead of identifying with the content of the movie, you become aware that you are the witness, the observer of the movie. So you get out of the melodrama. If you think you're one of the figures in the movie, you get sucked into the movie, right? You get sucked into the drama. And you start having feelings about these thoughts. All right; one step removed from identifying with the thoughts is me, my thoughts, is to realize that I am not the thoughts. I am the witness of the thoughts. I am the witness.

Next, step back, I am the observer. I am the observer, the witness. It isn't the thoughts; it's the experience of the thoughts. So you're the experiencer, witness-observer. What is it that's witnessing and observing? You're still going to call that odd, see. We're trying to get back from identifying with what's out there. First you think, "I'm the body"; then you think, "I'm the mind." I think, "I'm the thoughts." As you pull back, yeah, it's obvious that you're the witness, the observer, the experiencer. Now, try telling your mind to stop witnessing, observing. And you'll see that you can't, because that's not you either. Witnessing and observing is a quality of consciousness. It's not you. Everybody's consciousness witnesses and observes. It's an impersonal. So you see, what we're going to do is stop personalizing everything, and see that this is happening of its own. There's no volition on your part to be aware of what's going on. You don't have any choice in the matter. These conditions are impersonal to witness, observe, experience; the content of mind, to be aware of form, that's all impersonal. That goes with the hardware. So you draw back from being a subject in the movie, in the drama of what's happening out there, to being the witness of the subject that's experiencing it. In the void, you're part of the observer. And how does one know? How does the observer even know that it's observing? It's because it's conscious. So, you let go the identifications with all of that, and you see that consciousness is what is allowing all these phenomena. At this point, one thinks one is the consciousness. So you see, you stopped identifying with the movie; you're the witness of the movie, the observer, the experiencer. You move back to the awareness: that is consciousness itself that is doing this. Consciousness itself is impersonal. Awareness, then, arises.

The awareness that one is conscious—awareness is not something that you have any control over; it is not you either. That out of which consciousness arises is non-form, non-form. It arises out of a presence, it arises out of the Source; one moves back from the manifest to the Unmanifest—as a potentiality, the potentiality to be aware. In becoming manifest, one goes from the Unmanifest into the potentiality to become manifest, as the conscious awareness. The awareness is impersonal. It is the source out of which all existence arises. The substrate of all that is, one might say, that the allness of manifestation arises out of the Unmanifest, that which is the infinite source of the potentiality for existence itself—not even existence, but the potentiality for existence, is what Krishna calls the Supreme. It is the source as being not different than that which you are. The minute—as soon as this depersonalized one realizes, it is beyond all time, beyond all existence.

I realized that at age 12 in the snowbank. The presence came in with such impact of Divine exquisiteness, and the knowingness arises out of that field. The knowingness arises out of the field. The knowingness is so absolute. Henceforth, one knows on a level of knowing which the ego cannot experience. The ego can claim to know something. But it has no verification of its knowingness. It's a presumption. The ego can only presume that it knows; it doesn't really know that it knows. It has no confirmation. The presence renders an absolute authority that is absolute. The presence is so stunningly overwhelming, obvious, and it stops all thought; there is no question left to question. There is no "this" to question about "that." That which "is" is all that is. Therefore, there's no question to ask, because it's the absoluteness of self-identity. The absoluteness of self-identity is a little hard to describe.

One day the cat was sitting in the middle of the carpet, the absolute perfection of its cat-ness, the absolute perfection to the degree to which the cat was being that which it is, with no excuse, no explanation—just stunningly revealed itself. It just is what it is. And each thing can only be what it is. Except perfectly.

So one sees instantly the perfection of all creation. Everything is stunningly beautiful. There is no good tree or a bad tree. They are just equally perfect. And in that perfection is the innate beauty of creation.

Each thing becomes a living sculpture, each thing is a sculpture. And after that condition prevailed, walking down an alley in New York City, I saw, like an incredible painting by an impressionist, the garbage can all crooked over like this. And the garbage all lying there. And you see, you take an eggshell, it's an egg; you take an orange, and it's orange. You turn them all up and put them together and put them in a can, and now it's called garbage. It hasn't become different than what it is, but its appearance is different.

So then you see the perfection of all things, you know. And you see the tissue coming out of the Kleenex box is gone. And you see that it's like a Georgia O'Keeffe painting. You look at the Kleenex as it stands out there—incredible beauty as it stands there. You see its perfection, you understand? Its beauty is perfection. So beauty is, then, the perfection to which we can see a thing as it has become. In a meditative state—the reason it is said that this method is not necessarily suitable for the masses at this time is because when you decide to walk the edge of the knife, there can be no deviation. There comes an accumulation of spiritual energy, I think, from the heart. It is the inspiration of one's Love for God and for the truth—gives you the profound commitment, the same as to walk into a hail of gunfire for your country or be a kamikaze pilot, that level of commitment comes forth. Now every thought that arises, as it begins to arise, you surrender it to God. As you watch the thoughts arise, you will see they're like the waves of an ocean. The thought arises, it crests in its most manifest, complete form and dies away. You'll notice that the content of your mind is like music. No sooner has the note sounded than it is already fading, and the next note is already fading. And the next note. As this note arises, it is already in the process of fading, is it not? Which perception of the ego calls creation and destruction, you see? But you can see that's just an illusion. If you're on this side of the wave, you say it's creation; if you're on this side, you say it's destruction. Neither one. That's the dance of Shiva depending on which way you see it. The dance of Shiva, destruction and construction, is only a shift of perception, and on this side of the wave, it looks like it's creating, and on this, it looks like it's destroying. That's only how you're looking at it. You'll notice that the thought begins, the thought is arising. It's like a drive to think. There is an addiction to thinkingness. The ego thrives on thinkingness. The one thing the ego dreads is silence.

And it's true, what the Buddha said: that reality is glimpsed between two thoughts. That was very frustrating when I first heard that when I was young. Good, geez—how can you get between two thoughts? I tried to get between two thoughts. You can't get between two thoughts.

I tried to stop the mind so I could get to see between the thoughts, you know. I couldn't stop the mind. There, you'll notice you let go being interested in thriving off the drama of your thinkingness. Your thoughts are always creating a story—story about the past, what was, or a story about the future. So the reality, the subjective reality about which we're speaking, is in the split instant of now; the split instant of now is the source of the joy of your own existence.

It arises out of the moment, you see. That's always there. I have to sit on it, because—all right, one afternoon you say, "The hell with it, I'm gonna do it now." Okay. You sit down, you watch these thoughts. You see the thoughts are creating a story, and you're entranced with the story—the melodrama sadness of your life and the horrible things that have happened to you. And all the fears of tomorrow. And so you write a whole story, a whole melodrama of your life, and you're in love with it. Why are you in love with it? Well, because you're the star of the show, right?

It's your wonderful life. That it felt sad when your grandmother died and you lost your job and your cat was run over—I mean, God, you can work that one for a lot. And you got a terrible disease, and you only got three years to live, and you're getting old, you're going to croak one of these days. And now it's worrying you. You're running out of money and the rent's due. So you have to catch yourself that you are getting off on this melodrama, you're getting off on it, and you get a payoff out of it. And you have to be willing to surrender this to God. Therefore, the consciousness, Advaita, the whole Zen Buddhist practice, is really based on tremendous heart. You've got to have a lot of Love to be willing to let go the narcissism of this self-infatuation. Would I be willing to let that go for the Love of God? *"Almighty God, I do ask thee through thy Lord Jesus Christ and the Holy Spirit, to assist me in this endeavor."* And with great intensity, you start surrendering these things: "Would I be willing to let that go for God? Would I be willing to let that go? Would I be willing to let go of the enjoyment I'm getting out of this story?" All right, the story gets less and less.

I think the real knife that cuts through it is the heart. People like to separate the way of the head and the way of the heart, but it's only because of your heart in this matter. It's only because of the heart that you're willing to die for Jesus or die for truth or surrender your mind for truth; it's really coming from the heart. All right, so you're willing to surrender these thoughts. As you do this, you stop chopping the story, cutting the story short. You don't let yourself go all through your great-grandmother's funeral and all; you stop first in the middle of the recall. You say, "I'm not going to indulge in that." And then a new story comes up. The constant willingness to surrender it to God, surrender to God, to let it go, to let the willingness to let it not evolve into form, to not let it evolve into a heartrending drama—you've got to give up the heartrending dramas.

So you'll catch that: the mind is in the trick of juicing every story. It juices it for the melodrama, for the grief. It juices for the grief, for the anger, for the resentment, for the indignation, for the being right. It's the great juicer, so you've got to be willing to let go—the great mental juicer that tries to squeeze the story out. You either love God more than that or you love that more than God, so that separates the goats from the sheep. The willingness to go further is the willingness to sacrifice all that and let it go. So as the thought comes up, you let it go; as the thought comes up, you let it go. You see, as it begins to crest, it begins to take form.

There's two practices that would help you with this. You don't want to get caught by the thoughts. See, they've all got hooks on them. They've all got hooks on them, they've all got hooks on them. That's why the news annoys me, because they purposely put hooks on it. They're doing that to you. And it's so apparent that they're doing it too. It's not arising spontaneously. They're programming it, you know. There's two ways to train. One is, you see when you're riding in a car, you spot something along the road, and as you go along, your eye attracts it, right? It reads and looks at the billboard, it looks at the cow walking by, it's looking at the scenery, it's looking at the architecture—so your mind is tracking onto this and following it through, okay? That's what your mind ordinarily does. When you're looking at your mind, it gets onto a story; it follows the story. The way to train your mind—so, you'll sort of see what it's like—when you're riding in the car as a passenger, you pick a slot in the window through which you look, you understand? You look at the window right here; now everything is passing. This way you're not tracking it, see? This way your vision is caught by the subject of your interest, correct? You constantly go from this to that; that's how your mind is working all day. This catches it for a while. This catches it for a while. All right. But now you're going to practice something when you look through the window, and your project is to keep your eye at this place in the window no matter what goes through. Now stuff goes passing by. The difference is, you're not attached to it; you're detached. See?

You can't pull back to the mind so long as you're attached to its content and its emotional payoff. You witness the thoughts going by in meditation, you witness them going by, you don't allow them to take hold, you watch how your emotions want to come up and milk them for a story, for a kick. No, you refuse that. So you refuse the emotional payoff—every thought has a payoff, or you wouldn't have a thought. Every thought has a payoff. Every thought is a positionality, and you have a positionality because every positionality gives you a payoff—the payoff of being right, the payoff of being a victim, right? Every thought has a payoff. All right, so what you're letting go is really the payoffs, the emotional attachment to these thoughts. The images come up. As you do this, the willingness to let this go, let this go before the note even hits the crest, you've already let it go. You're not trying to hang on to it, because the new music is coming up, you understand? So you're staying on the edge of the knife, and as the thoughts come up, there's a letting go of it. So a feeling of, like, dogginess begins to arise, and you let it go before it even becomes good old Luke who got run over by the tractor. Yeah, you don't let the story get that far, your willingness to surrender. As you do this, you get more to the source of the thinkingness itself, and you'll notice the thinkingness is coming out of some kind of a primordial energy that is prior to form. Out of the formless energy, there's a desire and an addiction to thinkingness, which then begins to express itself as form. So as you start this, you have long stories. Then, as you keep letting the stories go, they become short paragraphs; then they become sentences. Then you let the thought go before it's even a sentence, before it's even a completed word or image, and you get that there is a source out of which all thinkingness is coming—the primordial, out of which thinkingness is arising like the lava in the middle of a volcano before it erupts and takes form in the world. You detect that that boiling wish, that pressure of thinkingness, is what you then surrender to God.

In an instant, all thinkingness disappears; the presence is all-prevailing, like a rush into the space created by the absence of the ego. That which "is" stands forth and is so stunning, you wonder how you ever paid attention to anything else. It then takes over the life, and it does whatever it does. To teach or not to teach, to give lectures, to write, has nothing to do with anything except that it does it by itself. The consciousness does that. The consciousness speaks of its own. I don't have to tell consciousness to speak; it speaks of its own. If it wants to demonstrate a Pollock painting, it does so. There's no thinkingness to it.

The one thing that made the mind useful for many years, there was no way to relate to the world. It didn't talk about anything comprehensive or sensible. The body went about its own business. There was no way to tell anybody what the condition was about. I never mentioned it until I wrote about it in '95. What do you do—walk down the street, tap somebody on the shoulder, say: "Guess what, I just discovered that the ultimate truth is the subjective reality of the Self as the All-Present Awareness of Allness"?

No, things just happened of their own. And it took a while to get used to the fact that everybody talks to the body and calls it this name. And it's always interesting to me, what's going to be said—I haven't the slightest idea what's going to be said. You hear it the same time I do. Wow. Sometimes it's terrific, you know. One thing it did do in how to relate to people was, it was very comical—the mind's response to some quality of humor, humor that seems to be innate in its compensation, because you could leave the world at any time once that energy comes to you; you're free to walk out of it. And one compensation I get for walking around and talking is this sense of humor. It comes up sometimes, it's so funny. And people will say, "You laugh at your own jokes." They're not my jokes; I have nothing to do with them. They came out of the blue fully formed in the way in which I got them. They break me up hysterically. I don't know where they come from. But sometimes the most funny things just appear, and they just appear out of nowhere and then continuously do that.

All right, so that pathway, direct through the mind, is how you get through surgery without anesthesia. It's also how you heal yourself of things. And people have watched it happen, where you fall down and you're injured, and the first thing you do is, you don't label it. You don't call it anything, like "sprained ankle"—the willingness to let go labeling it; the next thing is to let go resisting what it is you're experiencing. Next thing to do is let go calling it "pain." These are all labels and names. Radical reality has no names or form or labels. You don't call it anything. You let go resisting whatever has happened. You don't even call it "sensation," as you let go resisting the pain. The pain leaves your ankle and becomes general throughout your aura, it's equally present everywhere. You know the system is working, you let go resisting whatever you're experiencing. You don't call it nausea. You don't call it the flu. You don't give them a name like "allergy." You create all those things by labeling them. You give no name, you let go resisting it. As you do, you feel it in your whole aura. You continue to let go resisting it. As you do, it disappears and you get up and walk away.

So if you're having surgery and there's no anesthesia, I'll tell you: you walk the edge of that knife. The slightest resistance to the pain is excruciating.

As you continuously let go resisting the pain, you transcend it, like into an angelic space in which there is no pain; nor is there capacity to experience pain in the angelic realm. Yeah, so the angelic realm—is that an angelic realm? Yeah, that is an angelic realm. It was very aware that the Spirit was being uplifted by the angelic to a domain in which this physical pain was not experienceable. Anyway, that was just a side issue.

As you do intense spiritual work, all kinds of phenomena come and go, you know. There was a period of time when all the so-called siddhis, the siddhis came and went. There was—the minute you touched something, you knew exactly who it was who wrote it, where they came from; you give them their life story. That's got a name, I forget what it is. What's the name of that, do you know? Psychometry! Yeah. That came and went all by itself, and somebody's scarf was in my office back east, and I picked up the scarf. And I got it was "Estelle, my secretary," went out those thoughts. "You would have to have seen it. How did you know that it was mine?" I don't know. "It" said it.

So, it was psychometry. There was clairvoyance. There was distance viewing. I drove around states where I'd never been before, without a map, and drove directly to where I was going—all around Florida, where there's a million lakes in all. You just knew where to go, you hold where you are going to go and automatically, you drove there. There was all kinds of psychic phenomena. And you always knew what everybody was thinking. You were tele-pathic and all that stuff. All that came of its own. That's all the so-called supernatural, paranormal, psychic, what-ever you want to call it. It came of its own and it went of its own. Happily, I knew not to get attached to it, and I just witnessed it. You could fix electrical equipment—that still happens sometimes too. You just see it as being well. Amplifier is blown out, and you just see that the ampli-fier is perfectly fine. All of a sudden, the amplifier starts; then the person next to you says, "How did you do that?" I said, "Well, you do *A Course in Miracles*." He says, "I like that. Can I do the Course of Miracles?" I say, "I happen to have one volume—here." "Thank you so much!" And I never saw him again. So those things happen because of the energy of that aura, that particular energy level. Sick people get well; they come and sit down next to you and they're all crippled up and hallucinating and God knows what, and walk up whistling and feel fine. It's all gone.

You just witness it happen. It happens of its own. You have nothing to do with it. People who do *A Course in Miracles* have that same experience—that healing energy. I don't know what level that energy is. Let's see what that is; I don't know what it is. "That phenomenon was over 600: resist"—"that was the energy of the presence: resist"—the energy of the presence as what? The energy of the presence—Oh, "the energy of the presence as aura: resist." Okay, so the presence can express itself through aura. That aura was over 600, 650, 680, 690, 700. When your energy of the aura is around 700, it is capable of the so-called supernatural. Anyway, it's advised in all good teachings to not get involved with that, nor to pursue it for its own sake. Not to pursue it for its own sake because it gets to be an ego trip and you start to tell everybody that you're this, that, and the other thing. Also, it's not reliable. So these so-called scientific tests to see whether people have psychic phenomena are not real; the whole test is designed in such a way that it's erroneous. Those gifts come and they go; you can't just set up a laboratory experiment to see if you can count more fish in the bowl on the computer. It doesn't work that way. It comes and it goes. And the person has nothing to do with it. Those gifts come and they go; the gift arises because of some need within the world, and then it leaves. I remember once there was this lady waiting under the clock in the Plaza Hotel. She was clearly hallucinating—going on and on about somebody supposed to meet her under the clock. And I was quite aware it was a delusion, and God knows all this.

Anyway, the energy just prevailed. And pretty soon she got up happy, gave up the whole story, and walked away fine. So those phenomena happen, you see, but there's no personal self that chooses that. I think it says that in *A*

Course in Miracles too—that the healing capacity will arise from the need through the Holy Spirit; it has nothing to do with you and your willingness to be there. So sometimes you would feel like a transmitter—you would feel almost like a Divine energy going through you and coming out the heart, traveling somewhere and accomplishing some spiritual healing, I guess, and then the energy would stop of its own, you know. It had nothing to do with you; you were just sort of handy there. All right, so that's the way through consciousness itself. To understand the nature of consciousness—we'll get more into the content of consciousness when we look at positionalities. So, the big thing that creates the block is the propensity of the mind to take a position and then from that position, be in conflict about seeming dualities. I have to choose this or choose that—the so-called great block of the opposites, which at the highest level, is as I talked about before, had to do with existence versus nonexistence: "isness" versus "beingness" versus "goodness" versus et cetera. And the solution to that, then, is that there is no opposite to God. Truth prevails as it filters down. Humankind is like the forest for the trees and the leaves in the forest, so the sun is very bright and then as it filters down, it filters down and it becomes darker and darker and gives our society its form.

Muscle Testing: A Logarithmic Scale

How can you calibrate an archangel? Well, that has to do with calibrations. When you calibrate something, you say "on a scale of 1 to 1,000." You can say on this scale, or you can make up your own scale. You do not have to use this scale. You can say "on a scale of 1 to 1,000, where 200 is dividing between truth and falsehood, this person calibrates at such and such." If you don't specify or hold in mind a specific scale, you can come up with any number. See, scales are by agreement. "On a scale where water boils at 212 and freezes at 32, the temperature of this is so-and-so." But you could use any number, see? You can use centigrade or you can use Fahrenheit. You can make up your own scale; you don't need this scale. And people do, "On a pain scale of 1 to 10, this pain is what?" So, people have been using this map generally, you know, in reference to this scale, or they have a permanent intention that on a scale of 1 to 1,000, this calibrates at such and such as compared to this scale. So, let's do it again. "As compared to this scale, there are an infinite number of universes: resist"—okay (True). "There is that which could be called an angelic domain: resist" (True). "There are, within the angelic domain, beings who calibrate less than 600: resist" (True). Yes. There are very good spirits that calibrate in the 500s. You know, the angelic domain is not all just super angelic. If you get run over on a motorcycle and go out of body, you really want a friend, you know what I'm saying? You don't need a great guru there to say, "You realize that you are the source of the ultimate truth of the universe," you know? Right then you need a pal, I tell you. I mean, my jaw just got torn off, and I got a wife and kids, you know what I mean? You need a pal. So, "A lot of people are just good pals: resist" (True). "A lot of them are just the same as good pals on this level: resist" (True). Okay. All right. But then when we start getting into real power, real power in relationship to this scale, an archangel is over 25,000, 40,000, 45,000, 49,000. In relationship to this scale, we would calibrate an archangel at 500,000, over 500,000. All right, calibrate this scale. Yeah, compared to this scale. Now, this is a logarithmic scale. So the greatest beings who ever walked the earth calibrate 1,000. Now you're not talking about log 1,000, you're talking about log 50,000.

Generally, the paths to God are described as through the heart and through the mind. You can see that they are combined. You have to love the way of the mind enough to go through the sacrifice, because once you get on the edge of the knife, you cannot stop. The other thing about spiritual work that people don't understand is, it's not just a sporadic thing you do now and then. When you decide to "go for it," you are on the edge of the knife, and you cannot stop. This is *it*. You let go and surrender everything. Every tone as it arises is let go of. You're not going to sit back and enjoy the melody of the symphony, because as the note arises, you've already let it go, you see. You would have to hold it to compare it to the other notes in order to get music out of it. You hear the sound of the music, but you're not going to hear the music. You hear the sound, but you're not going to hear the music. You're going to hear the tone. Can it be done? Yes, it can be done, you see, because the real energy behind the Love is joy. It isn't just the Love of God; it's the joy—which *is* the Love of God manifest within yourself as the joy of spiritual work. So, the real energy that gets you going and keeps you going is the joy of spiritual work itself. Each instant is the source of its own joy, so you have no need for anything out in the world. Joy arises from the awareness of the Divinity of your existence in this moment. Therefore, as you walk the edge of the knife, you are outside of time. Time is irrelevant when you're on a tightrope. Time, space, all the stuff that the mind usually plays with is no longer relevant.

The other analogy I use for it is like the prow of a ship. See, the prow of the ship is consistent, no matter what the wave, no matter how high the wave, no matter what the wind. It's called "one-pointedness of mind." So, that one-pointedness of mind is a fixity of intention. It gets its energy from the surrender, the devotion to the joy of the presence of God which you intuit, but which does not become a stunning awareness until the mind disappears.

In theta, the background being that which you are, stands out, and the form is sort of translated. It's when somebody speaks—see, what prevails is the silence; then this form comes about. Somebody's mouth opens, and all this form comes out—I don't know what they're talking about—and there's a slight delay, and then there's a know-ingness of what is said. The Holy Spirit acts as a trans-lator. "That's a fact: resist" (True). You are, like, hard of hearing and absent-minded. And you're not always sure where your body is in space, but with practice, you get bet-ter at maneuvering it. So, there are physiologic changes. There's no need to eat. There's no need to eat at all. Today I didn't eat anything and I didn't even notice it, but I tell myself that for the survival of the body, at five o'clock, you should eat something, or thereabouts. Frankly, I could do without it.

So, there's no desiringness for things. Everything is complete and total at this instant. Therefore, because every instant is completely fulfilled and completely total, if something stops right there, there's no loss, because it is, at all times, continuously complete, you understand? If the doorbell rings, you can drop the piece of pie and never go back to it and don't miss the last half of the piece of the pie, because every bite of the pie is equally fulfilling; there's no better or worse. So, there's physiologic changes. There's a loss of startle response. A ton of cement could drop right behind this body, and it wouldn't even notice. Well, it would hear it, but it wouldn't react to it. The lack of the startle response is a slowing down of the brain waves. There is not being run by physiologic processes. And there's a long period of adjustment which required leaving New York City, where the life was quite complex, and moving to a very quiet place and getting adjusted and used to it all.

CHAPTER 4

The Greatest Resistance to Spiritual Progress

What holds up spiritual progress is resistance. You can presume that it's going to go on its way, because the ego, as I have explained before, has a vested interest in positions: I mean the vested interest in being right. Do you know what I mean? "Hey, I'm right." People are willing to die for being right, so you're not talking about something that's mild. The ego would just as soon see you dead as long as it remains right. It kills people right and left every day, doesn't it? Rather die than say you're wrong. The investment that the ego has is its own survival. The ego is not interested in your survival. Did you know your own mind is not even interested in your own survival? It would put you over the cliff anytime it wants to, to prove a point. It's not your friend; it is interested in its own narcissistic self-satisfactions. Its prime satisfaction, its prime delusion—the main resistance is—the narcissistic core of the ego is its belief in its own sovereignty. Becoming enlightened is really overcoming the claim and the domination of the ego to maintain its sovereignty. It will maintain its sovereignty at the price of your physical life. It will put you to death anytime rather than let you become enlightened. The refusal to accept that God is the sole source of all that is, is the ego's—the ego would like to tell you that *it* is the originator of your movements and actions.

If we look at the ego—I think in the last book, I did a pretty good job of describing the ego. The ego maintains the illusion of sovereignty. What do I mean by that? Well, the ego's functions are very complex. The ego has to sort millions of bits of data continuously, in milliseconds. It's processing all that you've ever known, all your perceptions, all your belief systems, comparing it with past calculating, and it's an extremely complex and incredible mechanism. The ego presumes that there is a central office to its functions. The ego has all these complex capacities, memory, comparisons. You look at a zebra; instantly, your mind compares it with every other zebra you've ever seen. A TV thing about zebras comes up—the camouflage value of black and white, and the fact you think it's BS. All this passes through your mind; it's all sorted. The ego is a very complex operation, extremely complex. No way a computer can even get near imitating it. Artificial intelligence can only take a small strand of it, which you can follow with logic and within differential calculus, but it cannot go to the nonlinear domain, because the nonlinear domain, by definition, is not knowable in a sequential way. This complex ego function presumes a central control office. This central control, with all its massive functions, like the central command, is presumed to be the "I." Hmm. At all times, the ego claims to be the author of all these phenomena. When a person says, "I," what they're talking about is the central organizing core of the ego. This central organizing core, like the Wizard of Oz, is behind the screen and manipulating all this stuff and claims to be sovereign, sovereign. *It* is God. So, the person then claims credit and takes the blame because it's claimed that the "I" is responsible. The giving up that illusion is what the ego fights to the death. And it's really: "Who is sovereign, God or the ego?"

The resistance is surrendering this illusion of sovereignty of the narcissistic "I" of the ego and realizing that your survival from moment to moment, everything you do and think, is a result of the presence of the Self with a capital *S*. The small self claims credit, but it's the greater Self that is the great sustainer of your life. I caught the ego doing that. I caught it. One time a rabbit ran in front of the car. Instantly, the brakes stopped, and I caught the ego claiming credit for saving the life of the rabbit. It claimed that it made the decision to put the brake on and save the rabbit's life, but it had happened already—I caught it. It was that split second the Buddha was talking about. Let's see how long that split second is.

"That split second is 1/10,000th of a second: resist" (True). "It's more than 1/10,000th of a second: resist" (True). "It's 1/20,000th of a second: resist" (True). I can't follow my words. "It's 1/5th of a second: resist" (Not true). Hahaha, "1/10th of a second: resist" (Not true). Anyway, it's a small fraction; the hell with it. I told you, the days when I had read about the Buddha and enlightenment was the space between two thoughts. I was trying to catch that 1/10,000th of a second. Well, no matter how fast you are, you can't catch that 1/10th second, because it left. Just as you are reaching for it, it's gone already.

So, the essence of resistance is the ego's insistence that it is the arbiter, the arbitrator, the source. Yes. This had to do with why we were talking about eliminating causality as a basic structure of the ego, because the ego is always claiming that there is an "I," this ego claims that it is the author of all your thoughts, et cetera. If you meditate the way I was explaining, you will notice that there's no author at all. This is all happening of its own. There's no author of your thoughts. They're just going by themselves, like a computer that's gone crazy. There isn't any "I" behind the thinking. There isn't any decider behind the deciding. The actions are happening of their own. We've said that everything is merely that which it is, expressing its potentiality as it comes out of creation. Was there an "I" that just decided to make up that sentence? No. The sentence spoke itself in response to the energy in the room and the prevailing electromagnetic gravity of the Presence of God. In response to somebody's thought, comes forth as those words. It has nothing to do with this person. There's no person that's here. There's no doer behind the doings. There's no thinker behind the thought. There's no speaker behind the thought; the thoughts are thinking themselves; the thinking is speaking of its own, you understand?

There is nobody "deciding" to breathe. Nobody in this room is deciding to breathe at all. That breathing is happening of its own, is it not? All these phenomena occur of their own. A person says, "Well, without an ego, how would I survive?" You would survive very well, because you survive in spite of the ego and not because of it. We're all alive in spite of the ego. The ego would have you think, "If it wasn't for me, you wouldn't be alive, man. You wouldn't get your flu shots or anything. I'm the one who is saving your life." No, because our survival comes out of inspiration, and that inspiration comes out of the Divine Presence, which automatically selects that which is necessary. All of that is happening of its own. It's all happening of its own. There's no thinker behind the thoughts; there's no doer behind the actions.

A Helpful Tool: The Thymus Thump When in a Panicked State

If you're caught in an emotional emergency, the best way to do is to breathe the energy up from—usually, it's your solar plexus that's in a panic. Breathe the energy of your solar plexus up to the crown chakra, and while you do that, go, "hahaha, hahaha," while thumping the thymus, and the sound of "mm." As you breathe the energy up, you're out of the panic right away; you're out of the upset. I am going to do this with the microphone. You thump over the thymus gland. The thymus gland is the controller of the acupuncture system and the immune system. It's right behind the breastbone. The sound "ah" makes you go strong with kinesiology, as does Love. So if you want to come out of a bad energy state, you think of somebody you love and you go, "hahaha, hahaha, hahaha," as you thump the chest. Now, if I test you with kinesiology, you'll go strong.

So, in the book *I* that I'm just finishing, the next-to-the-last chapter is called *"Homo spiritus."* So, man came up *Homo erectus* that calibrates only at 70. Then we come into *Homo sapiens*. *Homo sapiens* for many millennia were the Mongol hordes; everybody was savaging everybody else. So, all that *Homo sapiens* did was sort of a refined dragon themselves. Whether a Mongol horde or Tyrannosaurus rex is your preference, it wouldn't make much difference, would it? They were pretty much the same.

Then, we see the evolution of Love and progressive elevation of the level of consciousness. The presumption is that the destiny of consciousness itself as it expresses itself in man, man becomes born spiritually, and he is no longer *Homo erectus*, he is no longer *Homo sapiens*; he's now *Homo spiritus*. *Homo spiritus* is a different animal than *Homo sapiens* or Cro-Magnon man. He's a different person altogether—not the same at all. There's an awakening of reality on a completely different level. The nonlinear, the energy of the Spirit now begins to prevail as a motivator, as a goal, as a destiny, as a guide. The Neanderthal was not guided by that; there's no spiritual awareness in our definition of spiritual.

So, once you cross over 200, it seems that a new era has dawned upon the planet. The evolution of consciousness—you cannot predict the future, but we can predict what is the nature of consciousness itself. "Consciousness is created in such a manner that of its own 'what it is,' it evolves: resist" (True). So the progression of consciousness is not due to mankind. God doesn't need you as co-creator of what's happening on the planet at all. It's the nature of consciousness itself, and the common view is to return to its source.

I want to clarify the explanation we had before about *co-creator*. *Co-creator* indicates "two": there's this, and there's that. *Co* means "two." Mankind is not really a co-creator in the meaning of two different entities. God doesn't need you as a co-creator at all. What it means is that the essence of that which you are, because you are created as a seed of God, you contain the same seeds as God and have the power of creation. So you are not co-creating with God, you know, like in tandem. Do you know what I'm saying? God doesn't say, "Gee, I need help here," to take something to his planet—no. You are, because of the Divinity of your source, the extension of the lineage of that out of which you're created, and therefore you have the same powers, depending upon how spiritually advanced you are.

What You Hold in Mind Tends to Manifest

Somebody once asked me about the severity of menopause. You see, the mind is so powerful that what you hold in mind tends to manifest. That's a pretty well-known generality. The whole *A Course in Miracles* is based upon transcending that illusion that you are at the effect of anything out there. So, the persons having severe symptoms of anything, menopause being one of them . . . the prevailing belief systems about menopausal systems are sufficiently strong as to guarantee your developing menopausal symptoms, just out of the fact that you automatically will pick up that belief system from our culture. There's no way to avoid it. You turn on the TV, and there is somebody pitching something for menopause. So even if you don't believe in menopause, you sure will if you hang on to our society. That prevailing thought form, then, you give belief to it. The truth is, and I think the *Course* is very excellent in that, once you get beyond about Lesson 76, you realize that you are not at the effect of anything out there. Nothing out there has any power over you. Unless you believe in menopause, you cannot get menopausal symptoms. You say, "Well, I don't believe in that." Yes, you do. Unconsciously, you're holding that, or some aspect within yourself is holding that, as the truth. Because of that, it's manifesting. I always tell people who have illnesses of one kind or another to do *A Course in Miracles* and hope for the best. Hahaha. Because you do not know what your karma is. But if you advance to a high degree, you can transcend that karma and you won't even be subject to that.

Karma is a whole area for investigation. In kinesiology one of the neatest things about it is, you can ask questions about whether you got it in this lifetime, or did it come from elsewhere. "Everybody is mean to me." Why do you suppose everybody is mean to you? Well, because if you were once mean to lots of people, they've just been hanging out on the other side waiting for you, and now they're getting even. So all you can do is try to correct that karmic propensity. Those are only propensities; karma is only propensities. Sometimes it's so exact in its manifestation that you wonder—it seems like more than a propensity. In the middle of that surgery I had on the groin, they did a hernia operation with no anesthesia. I knew, and in fact, I saw the guy and know exactly what I did. I saw what the error was, and I saw this was the undoing of it. In my strict superego conscience, only by experiencing what he experienced could I right the karmic wrong that I had done. Out of what I took against myself as spiritual cowardice—I didn't have the courage to finish the job.

▲ ▲ ▲

Now, is there a physiological response when an angel comes into your aura? In the earlier stages, the experience I had was a tingling, like a tingling—no, it was like a flow of energy going up the spine, going up your whole back. It was exquisite. It was a sweet—like a low-energy—orgasm, almost. It was exquisite, and it just was continuous, and it went up the back, and it seemed to go up the spine into the brain. And in the brain, it created a sweet, incredible sensation. And if you focused over on this side, the sensation would focus to this side of the brain and this other side of the brain. And then it came down, and the experience was that when you went by something that needed some kind of spiritual help—probably a group of people praying, or something—this energy was so exquisite, it would go out the heart and go to that automobile accident, or people about to have a fight, or a couple arguing in the subway train, or something. It would go there and then sort of accomplish its purpose, and the people—the argument would stop, and all of a sudden, the energy would stop. So, that was that kind of energy. That kind of energy disappeared eventually. And, so long as consciousness remained stationary, there was no problem, but I think you can get tingling and all kinds of sensations. And as I told you, as it got further, any kind of error within the aura was exquisitely painful.

The Power of God's Grace

What about grace, the power of grace? Grace is—it's almost like the letting go of the sovereignty allows that which *is* sovereign to intercede. We call that intervention via the Holy Spirit, generally, right? That through contrition, through undoingness, through surrender and willingness that we create the space for the miraculous, which occurs as termed as "grace." Enlightenment itself is by God's grace, because all you can do is remove the impediments. You can only remove the impediments to higher consciousness; you cannot cause higher consciousness to happen. You can remove the impediments to Love, and then Love takes over. Love, having a higher energy, tends to transform the event itself. So, we can remove the impediments, but the final step is by God alone, you know. God only. That, we call "Grace." "Grace" means that, to our degree of knowingness, we could not possibly justify within any kind of reason the reprieve at the last instant, even though you know you committed the crime, and yet suddenly the reprieve comes through. Some people say it's the earned good karma from other lifetimes.

CHAPTER 5

Intention Is Very Powerful

What is the function of wanting something better in life? If we feel that something which somehow gives us the notion of the things that would be better, it's not necessarily a high spiritual thing, but just something we seem to naturally want, and then it brings that wanting: focus on it. It often brings with it, I find, also then the higher vibration, even though it's something that is not necessarily spiritual. Isn't it those vibrations which push us along?

It isn't necessarily following a higher vibration. Intention is very powerful. If you remove all the blocks to intention, it's possible to manifest things that would not otherwise be manifest. That was one of the basic teachings of EST [Erhard Seminars Training]. EST was very big as a weekend workshop training back in the '70s. EST would never allow you to have an excuse to be late. If the class started at 8:00 and you showed up at 8:02, you had to stand there until you admitted that you chose to be late. So the person would say, "Well, there's traffic, and there was this and that." All these excuses. Until you finally accepted that the reason you were late was because you chose to be late, they wouldn't let you in the door. Hahaha. Why? Because you rated something higher than being on time. So, you actually chose that you would rather sleep late than leave early enough to make sure that no delay would get in your way. Responsibility.

So, intention: if you remove all the blocks—the ifs, ands, and buts—in there, and if you remove all the excuses, intention can be very, very powerful. It's not that it's a different energy or vibration; it doesn't show necessarily a move up the scale of consciousness, but it's much more likely to accomplish its objective. That's what prevails when I catch chickens. Nothing stands between me and catching the chicken. It's like a clear channel opens between me and the chicken, and this energy shoots through that opening. That's why I would never engage in karate again or any of those things, because once you've got that space, you would just kill the other person in an instant. There's no way they can stop it, because all considerations are removed; therefore, the power shoots through you, and it's the power itself that accomplishes it. Death in one blow would be a snap. So intention, then, is what accomplishes the seeming impossible—dedication. That intention, that dedication, is what I was talking about when you walk the razor's edge. When you let every thought go as it begins to come up—the willingness to surrender it. Those of you that are in 12-step programs, it would feel like you take the third step on every single impulse, thought, feeling, as it arises: the willingness to surrender everything to God. And that is coming out of the heart.

Somebody's been diagnosed as having an illness. Well, in this case, it has to do with attention deficit disorder. I'll give you a practical clinician's diagnosis of—definition of how to diagnose ADD and ADHD. I've had 50 years of clinical experience, and right now, I've probably got three or four hundred patients with these disorders. As a pragmatist, ADD or ADHD is whatever gets better with Ritalin. They'll have all kinds of fancy things they want to do—psychological testing; it's usually an attempt to milk the parents. There're therapists for ADHD—good luck. It's a neurologic condition; it's genetic. It's due to the fact that in the precentral gyrus, we have suppressor strips. When you cut a chicken's head off, it goes crazy, right? So the motor neurons automatically respond via the spinal reflex, except that there're descending tracts that suppress it. These are coming from suppressor strips in the precentral gyrus in the brain, the premotor gyrus. The suppressor strips—if it wasn't for the suppressor strips, your bodies would all be going in every which way, see, because you're just dealing with a spinal reflex. It's only because of the suppressor strip that this doesn't jerk every time I touch it; every little breeze that goes by would cause a spasm in response.

So, the ADHD person is responding constantly to stimuli that our suppressor strips hold down, see. They're always restless, they're always jumping around, they can't keep their mind on one thing because of their distractibility. What Ritalin or some medication like that does is stimulate the precentral gyrus so it activates the suppressor strip. So, what would be a stimulant to a normal person is a sedative to them. It's also used in old folks' homes. A lot of old folks' homes, black coffee puts them to sleep because the suppressors—the sleep center of the brain is underactive. So you stimulate the sleep center, and *wham*, they go to sleep. So, anybody who has ADHD, you use what is a trial dose of Ritalin. Instantly they get better within an hour. They'll tell you: "I can sit still; I can focus; I can think; I can behave. I can mind when you say, 'Don't slam the door.' I can remember to not slam the door." That diagnoses it. Whether there's better treatments or conditions, I don't know.

The kinesiologic test, you know, is a tentative test. I would test it and say whether or not this person has it or they don't have it. If they have all the symptoms, though, I would certainly do a trial of it. Why? Because an untreated case of ADHD then compounds itself. The child can't behave, so they begin to get a self-concept that they're bad, other people don't like them. They feel the school is against them. They lose their interest in learning. They drop out and hang out in the streets and do drugs and start robbing ministores. So, untreated ADHD is worse than misdiagnosing it. The worst thing that can happen is—if you don't have ADHD—is, if you take Ritalin, you will be nervous for about an hour or two, like you drank too many coffees. It's better to diagnose it and treat it. And then, if there's behavioral means of overcoming it, God bless them. I've never seen it happen, but they could. Everything's possible to God, right? I've never seen it. It's more of a political position than a clinical reality. There's nothing wrong with having ADHD, except if it's untreated, you get all kinds of negative feedback from society, and that has the worst effect.

A Call for Help

There is a great variety of healing techniques as there are spiritual techniques that calibrate within the 200s. That doesn't mean they're not as good as something that calibrates higher. It means that it is addressing a different domain. Reiki, I think, and many of those things calibrate in the high 200s. What's important is whether a thing is integrous or nonintegrous. Reiki doesn't promise to take you to Enlightenment. They don't make that promise. They just tell you, "We're going to put positive energies in place of negative energies," or whether there's absent energies, or whatever. I would just say, you know, if I had this disorder, I would say, "Is this Reiki therapist over 200?" Yeah. "This is helpful, or Reiki is helpful to my condition, yes or no?" The hoped-for progression is to go from a lower level of consciousness to a higher level. We presume that almost everybody involved in spiritual work has that design in their mind that all religion has.

Well, historically that is not always a fact, due to errors. Can a person make a mistake and go down? Yes, just like the miraculous can occur and you can go up. When I got hit in 1965, it was "*kcck*," like that, it was just in one instant—total transformation. The mind was dead, the ego was gone, the person was no longer there, and there was only the startling magnificence of all of creation. Yes, in one instant.

The touch from the archangel which was the modus of the transformation of consciousness came as a response from the pits of hell. Just as you move up toward the heavens, form becomes less and less dominant and finally becomes formless. The descent into hell was similar. The descent into hell came after a long period of hopeless illness despondency. I'd been an atheist for years. I'd looked to philosophy; I'd looked to all kinds of things for the meaning and significance and the truth to the core of life. And was unable to overcome the illness or find any kind of meaningful spiritual truth. I'd already gone through theology, and I saw its intellectual dimensions and limitations. Anyway, there came a period of slow descent into hell. There were all these tormented beings and, I suppose, torture chambers and screamings and agony and dismemberments, and it was horrific.

That's what everybody thinks hell is—whoa, man. That's just jacks, for openers. This is just game playing.

It gets far worse. It becomes progressively formless. The despair now comes from such powerful depths that they were never suspected—that the depths were that deep, that profound and pitiless, and hopelessness and despair, and in leaving the world of form, I remembered, just like in Dante's *Inferno*, I saw a sign (it wasn't like a painted visual sign), but a knowingness. It said: "Give up all hope, ye who pass here," or something. Because there's no coming back. And the descent became worse and worse. And the agony became the agony of no hope throughout all of infinity. You understand, in the timelessness it was nonlinear, but like the negative side of nonlinear: beyond form, and again, purely subjective . . . it was a radical subjectivity of the other end of what the nonlinear domain of Enlightenment would be. In this pitch-blackness of hopeless despair, the agony was indescribable because it was of the spirit. And it was in the domain of . . . just like the highest level is beyond all time, it was beyond all time. Because it's beyond all time, there is no time in which it could come to an end, and therefore it was forever. That was the foreverness of hell. It isn't hell; it's foreverness. There was no hope of ever—and at the depth of all that, the atheist said—something in the atheist said, "If there is a God, I ask him to help me." I didn't hold my breath. Then everything went blank.

Then, a day or two, a day later when I came to, there was everything transformed. So, that call came out of the depths of hell. I think I did warn of that. The level was so deep, it took an archangel at 50,000 to go there—you would have to have very enormous spiritual power to persist and walk in and walk out of that—and took me with it. I forget what that was an answer to; it was something.

There's a curiosity that we've noticed, and it's only in the last year that we've really been looking at it: that people will calibrate higher early in their life than later, or vice versa. People make a profound jump, and jump hundreds of points in a vertical direction. I noticed some extremely well-known gurus, and when I would calibrate their level, they were like 200 and something; some even below 200. I said, "How can a well-known guru, worldwide fame, calibrate at that?" It's not believable. Sometimes the writings would be in the high 500s, and yet the being was only 190 or . . . I couldn't understand it. Then I saw, and I knew then from my own experience, what had happened. In a very advanced state, there came suddenly a knowing-ness—it's what I call a confrontation with the opposite. It's like when you reach a certain level, the power of that on the planet is a challenge to the satanic, Luciferic energies. And one almost summons forth one's opposite.

It once happened through a teacher who had been in high space and now came down. He wanted to charge for a certain teaching. I said, "Teachings are gifts from God; you can't charge for teaching. You can charge for the hall; you can charge for the food." I said I would like to teach this to all the priests—think of all the monasteries and seminaries where people are battling sin, and sin is noth-ing but an attachment. If you let go of the attachment, the sin disappears, because it's only an attachment to begin with. I wanted to give it away. All of a sudden, it's like the person was swept aside and the doors of hell opened up, and this horrid energy came through and started to talk in this crazy way that Jesus was just an astral and Buddha was just an astral, and it's no good unless people pay for it. It was bizarre, and the talking got even dumber. So, there's suddenly a confrontation with the opposite of wherever you're at. One time the energy came through— not through a person, not as an entity—through a person.

Oh yes. That was at a point where one had transcended personal karma. What was the energy of that field? Okay. "That was at, maybe oh, what, 700" (True). Yeah, around 700. The consciousness had advanced to a level where you calibrate around 700.

Suddenly there was like a confrontation, but not with an entity, because in the higher realms there are no entities, there's no angels, there's no spiritual guides; all that stuff doesn't exist there. But there was a presence. This presence was a knowingness saying through the knowingness, "Now that you have transcended personal karma, you are no longer answerable. There's no consequence to anything that you do. You have infinite power over all." One could then choose that power or not.

There's like a rarefied . . . it'd be like being in a high pass in the Himalayas, sort of, visually speaking. But it was a temptation. I saw who'd been through there. I saw that Christ had been there and said no. I saw a couple of people who you would call "fallen" gurus—I saw they'd said yes. It's like I saw everybody who had ever been through that pass, and I saw their choice. And I said, it cannot be used for personal gain and refused. "You mean, refuse all that power? You're going to refuse all that power, all that dominion over . . . ?" Anyway, so it appeared that a number of the famous ones—it also happens to nonspiritual people. It happened to Napoleon. Calibrate the level of Napoleon during his heyday when he was a military genius and on the rise. Napoleon calibrated about 450, right?

Let's see what Napoleon calibrates. "Napoleon, when he became emperor, the great conqueror of Europe, was over 450" (True); "455" (Not true). He was 455. All right. "Napoleon, by the time he was on Elba, calibrated over 200: resist" (Not true); "He calibrated over 170" (True);

"175" (Not true). He dropped from 450, which is enough to be the president of the United States, to 175. Why? Because his success had brought a megalomaniac power over others. And so, what happens to some of these gurus, which—I don't want to mention their names; some of them are world-famous, I tell you—and you calibrate their writings. Their writings may be 540, but that entity is now 190. Many of the highest gurus now calibrate in the low 200s.

What it means is fame, fortune, power over others, having many followers, becoming famous, having fancy titles, dressing in fancy garb, being called Baba "this" or "that"; eventually it summons forth the ego again, the temptation to spiritual vanity. So, it means in the beginning, they'd let go of enough personal ego to reach a good high personal spiritual state. That attracted many people. The person then still had unsuspected spiritual ego within themselves. My guess is they were unaware, unconscious that it was happening. It would be like you would begin to believe your own . . . ahhh, PR, yeah. Because there're well-known gurus still around Sedona—you mention their names, and everybody's, "Ooh, aah, ooh aah. Get outta here! Ooh, aah." So, you calibrate that entity now, and you see there's nothing to "ooh" and "aah" about.

So, it happens. It's a temptation. So, success happens like that. It can happen with Napoleon. It happens to movie stars. It happens to rock stars. People start out naively, but the wolf comes described in sheep's clothing, drugs, and immorality, that kind of thing. Luciferic is power over others, power over their minds, having many followers . . . Luciferic is the energy that destroyed Enron. They're not satanic; they don't want to cause anybody to suffer, you know, but, they have unprincipled greed for power.

So, the person as they evolve spiritually should be watchful of the spiritual ego. If one does it out of one's Love for God, you see—because of your Love of God, your consciousness grows. As your consciousness grows, it benefits all of mankind. Every living entity on this planet benefits from every single degree that your consciousness advances. So, you sacrifice personal gain. The Achilles heel of these fallen gurus is, they themselves were not trained by somebody sufficiently advanced to guard them against the attack from their own spiritual ego. A good spiritual teacher should warn the student. As you advance, your spiritual ego is naturally going to come in there, because that's the way it's designed. It's not that *you* are doing that. Therefore, you don't have to bother with guilt; you can just assume. If you write a good book and it becomes popular, your ego's going to come right in there. It's automatic. You just know it. Every time you win a game, your ego is going to come in there and say, "Boy, aren't you something!" You see, because the idea of a personal self still persists. A truly enlightened guru is not subject to that, because there is no personal self there to claim any gain. There ain't anybody there, nobody there that claims to be the funnyman when the jokes come up, you know what I mean?

So, the spiritual knowingness arises of its own essence. There's no personal self to take credit or for any gain; therefore, a person is safe if they no longer have any interest in gain, followers, money, wealth, influence. There was one guru that had, what was it, 99 Rolls Royces, or something? Anyway, he went down in flames. But if you test him out, that particular one—because he's so famous in Oregon—in the beginning, his teachings were quite high, and then he crashed down to a level. It was from having many followers, and . . . You see, the seduction of the Luciferic is very subtle. It's very clever too; it's very clever, and it deceives even the guru of that level: "For the good of your followers, you should really have all these to display the power of God manifesting as abundance." You know what I mean? You've heard that kind of crap on every spiritual street corner, right? How many workshops have you gone to since I told you that?

So, the difficulty with what I call the "false guru" is that the error is one of context, not content. They sound very erudite because the *content* is correct. However, the *context* in which this is presented is fallacious. The student is not that advanced. The student is not that advanced. The student is impressed with the content. And the level of the spiritual error is outside the level of the student's awareness. Very often it's out of the level of awareness of the guru. Even the guru is not aware that he's been taken in. Just got suckered in and is now serving Luciferic energies from other domains who are threatened by unconditional Love, unconditional Love. See, the wanting to give away a spiritual technique which would unhook all these—all these, um, monastic people—who struggle with sin and all that kind of stuff. I mean, this would have relieved them of all that suffering, and that would be a great threat to the Luciferic domain in this planet.

Consciousness Is Beyond Form

There are two different domains. One is consciousness, which has nothing to do with form. Consciousness is beyond form. The other is subject to form. The nature of the essence is like an acorn. Its innate essence is to grow and to prevail. If we calibrate the energy field of the consciousness level of mankind over the centuries, it prevailed at 190, century after century after century. See, one thing that kinesiology in spiritual research does is, it lends itself to research teams. If you have a particular interest, you can get together. We used to do this every Saturday morning, four or five people. We'd choose up teams, and we'd each one research a specific area. All I've done in *Power vs. Force* is to present, really, a new science, you might say. In each one of these, a change of even one point is very significant. But I had no time to do all that. All I've given is broad areas. You could go back century after century and see if there were any variations, and if there were, how much variation. And if so, associated with what, et cetera, and do other very specific research on that. I did not get the feeling, in going back over the centuries—but it was limited to the ones I did—that it was cyclic. I got it that it was progressive, that it constantly progresses, you see, but like a scale. One feather on this side tips you from this side of zero, and one feather over here tips you on this side of zero. You say, "Well, that's only one feather." Yes, but that's all the difference in the world, right? A laser beam being shot off a million miles off this corridor would pass some universes different than this, and it's only one feather. But that one feather is what our karma rests on, right? It's the one feather of, "Ah, let it go." Instantly, the feather went over on the other side. The sharp retort, you could have gotten even and hurt their feelings back, but you say, "Oh, the heck with it." That's the feather that makes the difference, yeah. So, you might say consciousness progresses at the rate of feathers. Every feather you let go affects all of mankind. Let's see if that's true, and then we're going to take a break again and then afterward, we're going to do kinesiology with the questions and answers, and we'll do interviews with people that traveled distances to see. "Every iota of spiritual gain, of spiritual progress, on the part of any individual affects the totality of mankind: resist" (True). Yes.

Every single, minute little feather that you put in benefits many elsewhere. Some child's lying there suffering in agony, and suddenly a feeling of hope comes in. That was your work that impinges on that child, who's now karmically earned the right to it. Without karma, there would be no explaining how it is, you see.

Everybody has a calibratable level of consciousness at birth. At the moment of birth, you're born at 300; you're born at 200; you're born at 600. How could that be, you see? Without understanding that consciousness prevails over huge eons of time, there would be no accounting for why it is that some are born with a calibratable energy of 45 and will probably not live more than six weeks and they will expire of starvation. And another comes in with a genius—Einstein—born that way. Usually, the consciousness does not advance much in a lifetime. People that become spiritually committed can go very rapidly. The average lifetime is maybe five points. You know, through trial and error, you learn the hard way not to make enemies. Maybe for a couple of lifetimes, all you learn is "don't make enemies." Nobody needs enemies in this world, let me tell you. Nobody needs enemies in this world. But it may take lifetimes just to learn that little thing, and here you just jumped five points, right? But even when you do, lots of people now feel pretty good that it's not smart to have energy in this world. They thought it came from them. No, it came because of you, that you put that out there, that that really works. So you help all of mankind with every spiritual movement you make.

▲ ▲ ▲

Can a person use kinesiology all by themselves? Yes, there's this so-called method which is described in a book called *MAP*, written by a nurse. People who are interested in kinesiology, there are sources that they can contact for much greater information. I'm not a kinesiologist. Kinesiologists are very often holistic health practitioners. Chiropractors are usually the best holistic chiropractors. We have a friend who does it constantly using this ring method. Does everybody know this method? Yeah, you hold it as strong as you can. Now you picture Jesus and try to pull it. Now you picture Bin Laden and try and pull it. You'll notice there's a difference in strength. So, kinesiology is really a difference in strength. That which is pro-life tends to make you go strong. That which is anti-life makes you go weak. Again, that sounds like a polarity.

In these gradations of consciousness, we start out from the Infinite. If you calibrate what is the energy—I'm doing this for the book I'm doing now—the various names for God. What does this name for God—what is the energy, the reality behind it? And it will say, "Infinite." The true names for God all calibrate out there as Infinite. There's a book that describes this particular technique. Then there are people who are professional kinesiologists, and they put out very excellent teaching tapes. They're much better at demonstrating it than I am. We have a friend who is a chiropractor, holistic practitioner, and as you're talking to him, he's checking out the calibrations of the energies of everything you're saying as you say it. And he's checking out your past karma about that. His fingers are going like *this*. He's, like, tracking everything you're saying and doing. "I think in one lifetime, you probably pulled your grandmother's arm almost out of the socket. That could have something to do with the guilt about that." And he's going on and on: "And here's what you can do—press these acu-puncture points. And here's the affirmation I'll give you: 'I forgive myself for losing my temper and injuring somebody I love,'" and et cetera. That's one approach to kinesiology. Mine is only to do research in spiritual truth and spiritual reality and try to devise an understanding of the whole evo-lution of consciousness throughout all of time.

We ran across the fact that there are multiple dimen-sions. This is only one dimension. There's an infinite num-ber of dimensions. Each one of them has their own reality. Each one has its own hierarchy. The astral domains—you can go to any spiritual bookstore, and there's all kinds of books channeled from all different domains. Within that astral domain, you'll see there's a whole hierarchy of beings and titles and they have their own gods, and these are by choice. These are by choice. Many people are repelled by Love and goodness and God and forgiveness. There are countries where it's actually illegal. In Cambo-dia, after Pol Pot executed anybody who was everybody, any public exhibition of Love or lovingness or forgiveness or mercy was illegal. It would get you put in prison.

The Nazis trained their soldiers to be totally immune to Love and tenderness and any consideration. You remem-ber this famous incident where the Japanese soldier bayo-neted the baby being held in the arms of its mother and felt victorious that he had perfected this satanic energy. So, the negative (what we would consider from a spiritual viewpoint), nonintegrous realms have their own integrity, where your status depends on your capacity to be unfeel-ingly cruel. The Japanese certainly exhibited that in Man-churia in the early '30s. They exhibited it in their treatment of the prisoners in World War II. There are domains which are the opposite of ours. To have compassion toward another is a weakness, and you are laughed at as a fool. You understand? The mirror image of ours. You see this in the Mafia, where you're not a "made" guy until you murder somebody with a witness. You have to, in other words, choose hell. Choose hell. Now, you have rank in hell. Um-hum. So, Adolph Hitler and Stalin and all those fellows probably have a high rank in the domains where they are, you know what I mean? To kill 70 million innocent people without feeling a thing, then commit suicide at the end. All right, that's how you get to be head of the Mafia in those realms. I don't know, it's probably choice. Choice.

Why is it that life can express itself in such a way? A couple of questions refer to that. There is no *opposite* to God. That which is not God is merely the refusal of God, but not its opposite. Now, we've said that those levels have to do with Love, so at the very top you have that which is infinitely loving. And as you come down, life just doesn't disappear; it takes a different form. Below 32 degrees, water turns to ice. Below 200, life turns into a different expression. That mollusk who stands for the most venomous thing I know of on the planet makes a black mamba go scared. You know, a black mamba is scared of that mollusk. It calibrates about 5 or something. Should we call that "evil"? I don't know. Maybe that which chooses that lifestyle thrives and feels good about it. It's choice. One can see then—don't forget, you're trying to escape the trap of duality—what you're seeing is the gradation of one . . . Just like there's light, and less and less light, there's Love and less and less Love. If you remove Love, then you have the self-servingness which we would call, from a psychological viewpoint, narcissism: the concern only for oneself and nothing else other than one's own desire. One way of understanding the ego and a way that gets you out of duality and the "make wrong" of the ego. The reason I don't like the textbook in *A Course in Miracles* is, it lapses. . . . The workbook is very good, and I tell people, do the workbook and ignore the textbook. Why? I used to be a spiritual teacher. I brought it to Sedona. I knew Helen [Schucman] and all the people involved. The textbook gets into a polarization with the ego, like the ego is the bad guy and you're the good guy, and your job is to conquer the ego. That's getting polarized with the ego, and that's going to strengthen the ego.

There is that which is loving. All right. Because one chooses a spiritual pathway . . . Don't forget, you've already made a decision based on a positionality. You've already come to a conclusion—a positionality that spiritual is better, right? Spiritual is better for *you*; that's *your* choice. Spiritual is not better for a black mamba. If a black mamba decides not to bite and kill you, he don't last long as a black mamba. So, life takes its various forms.

We could say that That Which Creates Life gives life complete freedom. "Life is created completely and totally free. We have permission to ask that: resist" (Not true); "Life is created completely and totally free. We have permission to ask that: resist" (Not true). We do not have permission to ask that. Once in a while, you get a no.

Stay with the Knowable, Not the Hypothetical

Do I give myself permission to have the freedom to live my life as I choose? Let's stay within the realm of the knowable, because some of the questions really deal with the hypothetical. Why is it that things that seem ungodly or devoid of Love, they seem to exist, and the answer is, "I don't know!" It would seem that one has a choice within one's own experience. You see that you're presented with possibilities to choose one way or the other. So, that's all we can say, is that by choice, one advances in this direction, or one chooses the other direction. The "why" of that, let's just get a definite answer on that one. "The why of it is because of the audience: resist" (True). "The why of it is because of the question: resist" (True). "The why of it is because of the intention: resist" (True). Something's very out about it, the intention. Oh, I know. "What I'm thinking is so: resist" (True). Okay. All right. So, it isn't something we need to discuss. You don't need to know it. You can become enlightened without answering the question. It's a hypothetical question. I'll get that into the next book.

Answering the question to what seems to be the polarities of good and evil is quite a conundrum. I mean, it has bothered man since the beginning of time, right? Because Eve didn't know kinesiology, we've all had a tough time. Had she calibrated the energy of that viper, life might be different, right? And so, there are unanswered questions. There are unanswered questions; why that should be, huh? Why that should be that way, we'll leave that for another book.

Now, can certain drugs cause people to go suicide? I can't say that a drug has the power to cause anybody to do anything. There are certain drugs that are alleged to have certain side effects and the exact reasons are not exactly known. Sometimes the clinical reason for it does occur later. There is a dermatologic drug that is alleged to drive people into depression and into suicide. But, you see, every step along the way, you have a choice. If you're depressed, you can go see a doctor about it. You can take an antidepressant about it. You can see a psychiatrist if you feel so depressed you think of suicide. So, you've got your freedom of choice. Usually out of pride, the person won't go see a psychiatrist and they kill themselves, but it's not really due to the medicine; it's due to the fact that they're too prideful to go and consult another human being about what their problem is. He probably could have cured him with Prozac. There are drugs that do have effects on the brain's neurotransmitter systems and can create quite a depression.

There's two kinds of depression. There's depression which is just serotonin and maybe noradrenaline in the brain, and then there's bipolar depression. Chemically, they are two different items in the brain. So, if the doctor thinks it is just plain depression and it's really a bipolar depression, if you put him on Prozac, you take him out of the bipolar depression and throw him into bipolar mania. The Prozac doesn't cause the mania. What it does is, it removed the depression, and now the mania. So, every patient that has to do with depression, I suspect they're bipolar depressed; they are possibly that, and if you just put them on an antidepressant, they may go into a manic state, see. So, it wasn't that Prozac drove people into mania; it's that it uncovered an undiagnosed bipolar condition. So, anyway, it doesn't cause you to do it, but it would present you with a situation where you might choose that.

Well, when we talk about the unfolding of the universe, this understanding of it is that intrinsic to creation is the power of creativity, so that that which is created has within it the essence of God, which may then continue to manifest as further creativity. In other words, it's innate to the universe by virtue of its creator. Now, what seems to be an unfoldment of the universe, you're talking about perception. From the viewpoint of Radical Reality, nothing is unfolding. That probably sounds like nonsense. From That Which Is, nothing is unfolding. There is nothing to be explained. An unfoldment would be a change, a moment; these are all selections of perception, which then seem to beg for an answer only if they're perceived as such. Inasmuch as, in the realm of the Absolute, none of that is happening, there is nothing to be explained. That probably doesn't make any sense. The Supreme Being is Unmanifest, unmoving, unchanging. There's nothing unfolding, nothing being revealed; it is as it is. Out of that Unmanifest arises the manifest in which perception, because it's sequential, sees things as happening and then looks for an explanation of the happening. There is nothing happening. Everything is just *is* as it is, huh? Even when I say "unfolding," what I'm really saying is, from the viewpoint of perception, it *seems* to be unfolding. From the viewpoint of a more Radical Reality, everything merely is what it is, because each instant is complete and total within itself and is outside of time. So, many of these questions only make sense from the viewpoint of time. I don't think that's a very good answer for the listener, because it cannot be explained. So, many things cannot really be verbalized. It's just the Reality as it is, and it's not explicable. Those are attempts by verbiage to address the question, but it doesn't answer the question, because there is no question—so there is no answer. That is not comprehensible, but it is so. Let's see, for our own sake. "That is so" (True). That is so.

That which seems like a question is a positionality languaged in the viewpoint of the ego, and because it makes semantic sense, it presumes there is an answer. From the viewpoint of Radical Reality, no construct within form is real, and therefore it is not actually answerable. Every question is unreal. It seems to be answerable at a certain level, but as you transcend that level, no question is possible, and therefore no answer is necessary; nor is it possible either. The best way I can answer that question is with a bit of nonsense doggerel, which probably originated in the 1800s in England: "Why is a whirling mouse? Because the more it spins, and then some." That, to my ear, is the sound of *all* questions. But they get translated into what I understand the human is saying by that, and therefore it's answerable. All questions are in the form of "Why is a whirling mouse?" when you examine them and take them to their roots. "Why is a whirling mouse? Because the more it spins, and then some."

Some things are not answerable. And if they are not answerable, one is not to decide that one doesn't know the answer. One is to decide that the question is not answerable. "Why is a whirling mouse?" I got the answer after 50 years of meditating on that koan: because it isn't!

A lot of people ask about specific spiritual organizations, techniques, workshops. The best thing to do with them is . . . Most of them are going to run in the 200s. Most of them are quite useful. Most of them lead to a greater understanding of human psychology and motivation along the way. Most of them provide the broad educational training that a person needs. To become spiritually evolved requires, really, in a way, a certain sophistication in our society at this time—in this lifetime. So, one is sort of getting a general education about the whole spiritual domain: what are its dimensions; what are the various avenues that people follow; sort of an understanding of humanity in its desire to know itself and to know the highest truth. One comes out from looking at all of it with a certain degree of compassion for all of humanity. The incredible lengths to which people go to reach God—prayer wheels that they go tens of thousands of time, people that sit decades reciting the same mantra over and over—the dedication, the profound commitment, is awesome in a way.

In the book I'm working on now, we calibrated a lot of these techniques: the Jesus Prayer, Om Namah Shivaya, Om Mani Padme Hum. They mainly are quite high—they are in the 500s. There's no doubt that if you recite a mantra that's in the high 500s, then the motivation behind doing such a thing is sufficient to drive one the whole way. In other words, there's no magic in the mantra. There's no magic in the mantra. A lot of these spiritual things get to be held in a magical way. No, the intention behind the prayer wheel, whether there's a prayer in the canon or not, as it rolls around and around probably has nothing to do with it—but the fact that anybody is willing to sit there and rotate that thing 10 thousand times for the good of mankind, that's enough to get you all the way into heaven, if I were the doorkeeper! A spiritual mesomorph has got all the muscle to rotate that prayer wheel. And the things that people do, you know, brings great compassion that man would be that interested in the Ultimate Reality and the desire to reach God; to do all the strange and what sometimes seem almost horrific things to reach the Truth is probably that which contributes to the salvation of mankind and brought Christ down to earth as a Savior to manifest the energy of the Savior. Mankind, in a way, let's say, earned it. Let's say, mankind earned the right to have the Buddha here and Jesus Christ and all the Great Teachers that have been here, by its own karmic merit and earned the right to salvation, huh. Mankind *en masse*, the totality of mankind. Are we all for that? Everybody? Vote for that? I vote for it.

Relationships and Levels of Consciousness

Is there a difference in the calibration in regard to relationships, perhaps between an individual that may calibrate above 310 and one that may calibrate just below or above about 200? Those levels there denote the general realms. The 300s have to do with willingness—310 is Willingness, a different energy altogether, than the ones below it. The ones below it are integrous. Willingness is already the beginning of Joy. To be asked to help with a project and to feel the joy of contributing to that project; to know that you are part of humanity by doing so, that you're assisting the people you love; it's almost like you acknowledge the family love of mankind. The willingness to be of service to others is already a very good advance. People in the 300s are great to be around. They're helpful, they're cheerful, they take responsibility for their own actions, they don't tend to blame things on you, and therefore they're very strong, very strong. They really build the nation, but they build it, you might say, to the degree on the willingness of the 200s to put forth the effort. The joy isn't there yet. In the 200s you don't experience the Joy. There's satisfaction, however, and there's a feeling of freedom. The level of Neutrality is 250. Neutral is a very comfortable place to be. For one thing, you've escaped the Fear and Negativity of the lower dimensions. With Neutral, it's okay if you get the raise and it's okay if you don't, so you don't worry. Down lower, you don't get the raise, you think of suicide or you go into a rage and go postal. "Go postal" is down near the bottom, there. Neutral, if you don't get the raise, you'd say, "Screw it. I lost a lot of money. What the hell, I'll make it back some other way." Whatever your financial karma is, you'll get it back.

Neutral people are easy people to be around. They're not vindictive; they go with the flow. Neutral is "you go with the flow." In Neutral, you're pretty self-sufficient and you're comfortable with yourself. Because you're comfortable with yourself, other people are comfortable with you. People are about as comfortable with you as you are accepting of yourself. The person who's totally self-honest and self-accepting never gets resentments, and they don't get their feelings hurt. There isn't anything that you can say about them that they don't know already, and it's okay with them. The way to disarm your opponent is to agree with everything negative he says about you and tell him that not only are you the best liar, but you're the best liar in town and you're worth a fortune. "You want to hire me? I can sell more Buicks in a day than you'll sell all month." Anyway, no matter what they say, you insist that you are a high degree of that. And immediately your opponent becomes disarmed. You understand that? It's like martial arts. As he comes with you this way, you go with him that way, and now his attack is weakened because he can only attack you if you resist him. So if they tell you you're selfish, tell them, "Selfishness is good. This world was built on selfishness. And when it comes to being perfectly selfish, I'm the king." Well, what can they say? You've already agreed with them, you've disarmed them. You know what I mean?

You see, in Neutral, they're out of Denial; 200 is the level of integrity. Integrity is the level of truth. You can't get sober in AA unless you cross the level of 200, because the first step in AA is, "I admit I am powerless over"—or any of the 12-Step programs—"I admit that I am powerless over 'so-and-so.'" Well, that's the truth. If you had power over it, you wouldn't have the problem, would you?

So, that's jacks for openers. So, 200 is jacks for openers into the spiritual world, where you're willing to admit the truth about yourself and you give up being defensive, and you stop being guilty.

People below the line are hard to deal with because they're very defensive.

So, 200 is Neutral, a very nice, comfortable place to be; 175, you see, people are prideful, and they get "tiddleyed" if they make any mistake. If you say, "You stacked the cards backward." "I did not!" And, "You told me that." You know, it's very defensive, so it's hard to deal with. Neutral is easygoing, because each Neutral knows that you can't live a day without making lots of mistakes—it's impossible. That person who didn't make a mistake today stayed in bed all day, and it was a mistake to stay in bed all day.

So, forgiveness comes in out of compassion. Compassion is really the answer to most of the lower negative energy fields: compassion for yourself and for others, the willingness to forgive, the willingness to forgive and overlook human error. Human error. Error is built into the human mechanism, and so error is inevitable. I just read a very good article out of *Fortune* magazine that most companies are designed for success and they have made no preparation for error. And they're discovering now that the company that knows how to turn error around in a very positive way is a far more profitable, beneficial, and friendly place to work. So in your company, what you do is, you set up your error strategy: "First of all, errors are going to occur here. How are we going to handle them? What are we going to say to the customer?" Et cetera. So, you get out of defensiveness and you turn it around into a positive. I thought that was a very beautiful article for *Fortune* magazine.

You see, a lot of what is really considered spiritual is quite acceptable in the world of commerce as long as you don't label it. As long as you don't call it "spiritual," it goes a long way, and of course it's very profitable on the bottom line. Spiritual principles are highly profitable to the companies that institute them, but they don't use spiritual terms or spiritual terminology which turns a lot of people off. The basic truth can be very profitable to any company. Certainly, to be considerate of the customer—I don't know how any of these companies make it that you call up and you get this string of answering machines, and then you punch 6 and 8 and 12. I mean, how much does a human being cost an hour? Nowadays you can get them for nine dollars an hour, right? I mean, you're this giant corporation, and you can't afford nine dollars an hour to have a human being say, "How may I help you?" with a really friendly voice? Wow. They're saving nine dollars an hour and losing millions by the hour; disgusted customers hanging up, saying, "I was on the phone for 20 minutes, and I never got a human being. To hell with them." What does it cost them?

So, the insensitivity of corporate life at its interface with the human domain is of interest to me. I recently got a call from a writer for the *Wall Street Journal* writing an article on that. The institution of spiritual principles in business: does it actually show up on the bottom line or not? To even ask the question seems, to me, sort of absurd, but you know the difference yourself: you get somebody helpful and friendly on the line. So, what you want is somebody who answers your telephone is at 310. In Neutral, "No, he ain't in now." It's okay with them to disappoint you, because their self-esteem doesn't ride on pleasing you. A person down below may be angry. An apathetic person—we get a lot of apathy on the telephone; those are about fourth-grade dropouts and the government has assured them some kind of a job, but they really shouldn't be in the workplace, actually. They need training on how to be in the workplace.

So, each one of these fields [on the Map of Consciousness®] represents a certain level of consciousness, which is impersonal. Each one of these fields, by our assent, tends to dominate the field. So, our thoughts, without realizing it, tend to be in tune with a prevailing energy field which we have brought in out of our own agreement. We call that *entrainment*. The energy field prevails in society, and by your assent, you agree to that energy field, and now it tends to dominate your consciousness.

We see that the success of the negative energy fields depends on that entrainment. And in that book, and the book I'm just finishing and research I'm doing now, it isn't the lyrics of certain negative kinds of pop music; it's the energy field which accompanies it, which is like a carrier wave. That carrier wave contains the pattern of that negative energy field. So, it's possible to unconsciously invite in a negative energy field to dominate your consciousness. You went to the party to have a good time, but when you walked out, you're now under the domination of a field which we could term "satanic," yeah. One has now agreed by propinquity, and the energy field now dominates that person's consciousness. So, all they did is listen to a lot of rock music and get stoned, and as far as they're concerned, that's just having a high time. And nobody sees the connection between that and walking into the schoolroom and killing eight people. You ask them on it, you see them on TV: "Why did you do that?" "I don't know, I just wanted to see what it felt like." He just wanted to see what it felt like. And how did the person ever get to that level of consciousness? Because their consciousness is dominated by a negative field.

So, these fields which we tried to calibrate, we can depict them with a generality. Don't forget, these calibrations are sort of general. In other words, I can't say that it's 200 or 201.2. Why? Because it's really a whole new field for investigation. One could spend a lifetime and a Ph.D. dissertation exploring just a few points above and below 200 and how that manifests in society. What does a jump in two points—from 202 to 204—how does that manifest in one's annual earnings? How does it manifest in job title? Even two points from 202 will take you from the back desk to the front desk, right? From 200, it will take you from the front desk; from 202, will take you to the manager's office. Another two points will take you up to be assistant manager. Probably another two points, you're manager. So, we're dealing in broad numbers, but I'm sure even slight variations have quite a profound effect as they express themselves in human life and society. So, each one of them is really a field for detailed research. What we've really done is sketch out the broad outlines, but we haven't mapped out every nook and cranny in the coastline.

CHAPTER 6

The Willingness to Completely Surrender One's Life to God

How far up the scale is it possible to go in one lifetime? From the depths of hell to the Presence of God, within a day, is a subjective experience, so that would be practically the whole scale. It's possible to jump enormously, because you don't know what kind of karmic loading is behind such a move. Understand what I'm saying? You don't know what the possibilities are. I think, by choice . . . Yes, I think I see what the answer is, actually; what I actually myself did and what Ramana Maharshi recommends, okay? "Taking the third step at great depth will take you all the way from the bottom to the top: resist" (True). What I did was what's called, in AA, the third step: "the willingness to completely surrender one's life completely and totally to God with no considerations, no withholdings, no matter what." Ramana Maharshi recommends to look within and ask, "Who am I?" He is not exactly correct. It's not "Who am I?" [It's] "What am I?" "Who," you're looking for a personage again—it's like you're looking for a bigger, better ego. So, I don't agree with that teaching as it is verbalized. "What am I," because the "what" is impersonal; the "who," you're looking, like, for a higher *person*.

Ramana Maharshi, you know, suddenly dropped over at age 15 or 16, whatever it was—he was just an ordinary

117

religious person, Hindu—and thought he'd died. And obviously in that moment, completely surrendered, and saw himself as dying and dead. And then came out of that experience at 700. And he never left the mountain. I know what he experienced, because in walking through, what should we say . . . in completely surrendering everything, there was the experience of dying—of great, profound anguish, of really dying. One knows that one is—really—dying. And you know you're dying, and it was, in this experience, rather dreadful. But it only lasted a few seconds, half a minute, something. But it was very, very definite, the experience of dying.

It's not possible to experience one's own physical death. Forget about experiencing your own death. Nobody experiences their own death. It's not possible to experience your own death, because you're out of body, and when the body goes, you're not there. So you don't experience any death, because you haven't died. How can you experience your death when you haven't died? But the death of the ego, yes, that is the death that people dread. They think it's the body, but it's the ego—one's identity. So, the willingness to surrender even one's identity as "I," as "me," to God can bring about enormous change. It was through that great space that the splendor of That Which Is shone forth. You never experience your own death.

There's two questions that we could do just as an aperitif. "We have permission: resist" (True). "One never experiences their own physical death: resist" (True). That's a fact. You don't have to worry about experiencing your death, because it ain't gonna happen. The other question that we sort of need to know—"we have permission to ask this one: resist" (True). "The time of your death in this lifetime is karmically set: resist" (True). It's karmically set, so why worry about it? The time is certain, and you're not going to experience any death anyway. One of the biggest reasons for the propagation of the ego is fear of death. To merely know that you're not going to die, you're not going to experience any death, and it's already set already, relieves a great deal of reason for the ego to continue its dominion over you.

That brings to mind a question about karma: so, what can you do in this lifetime to negate any karmic responsibilities that you may have acquired? Do you have any shortcuts? Do good at all times to all people and cross your fingers. I guess one follows one's spiritual direction to the best of one's ability, which is all that's required. You know what I'm saying? That's all that's required. It's not that God is a cruel taskmaster. See, God is not arbitrary. God is completely nonarbitrary. One earns one's way out by one's own good intentions. And you watch Dickens's *A Christmas Carol* every year. It's worth watching every year, because I think it's a great spiritual treatise. I think that Dickens's *A Christmas Carol* is one of the greatest spiritual treatises ever written. The Ghost of Christmas Past—we see where it would take us in the future, and now we have the chance to choose differently, that's all. He was a great spiritual teacher.

"The question is, are you free to move to their level of calibration, or do you help them move into yours? What's the bridge between the two?" You don't move your level of consciousness to match theirs. Out of willingness to communicate, one accommodates. The personality—what Jung called the *persona*—does that all the time. A certain type of languaging is appropriate for one group and it is not for another, so you do as the Romans do, for the sake of harmony. The persona, in this particular instance here, automatically adjusts to whatever environment it's with. It tends to not want to be around people who calibrate less than 200. It doesn't enjoy it much, any more than it enjoys loud noise. It doesn't enjoy it, but there's a natural willingness out of compassion to be what you feel you can be to others when it is appropriate. If it is nonintegrous, there's absolutely no reason to go along with it. One could merely disregard it. You know, Christ said, do not fight evil; just ignore it, walk away from it—to walk away from that which is not compatible.

At a certain level, one, for instance, may leave the big city and move to the country where it's very quiet. Now, the peace and quiet of the country would drive some people nuts. They come visit you for a day or two, and they can't wait to get back to the big city. They are attuned to that energy. One just does what one can to be compatible with others for the sake of harmony. You don't have to start giving them a lecture that bullfighting is wrong. Bullfighting calibrates at 35, by the way. Dogfighting and bullfighting calibrate around 35. It's about the same as the Roman Colosseum: blood for the sake of blood. You don't have to give them a lecture about that—that dogfighting is immoral, or something.

For the Joy of the Work

Now, if a spiritual teacher is not supposed to accept any money for the teachings, just for the facilities and food and whatever, how does the spiritual teacher eat? It isn't that they shouldn't; it's just that that's not a primary goal—not a goal, see. But naturally one has reality, needs that have to be met. So, what's appropriate? You see, all things that the calibrated level is, is all based on motive. What is the motive? The integrous teacher is not interested in whether one has lots of followers, lots of fame. You do it for the sake of the work. Because of the joy of the work. I have three radio programs coming up soon. The question is: Why should you do a radio program? Do I really want to do radio programs? Well, to have this kind of knowledge and not share it with others . . . In other words, to have certain knowledge that can be helpful to others, one gets joy out of sharing it. It would be like Sir Alex Fleming, who discovered penicillin. He excitedly ran all over the place. He'd say, "Wow, this can stop disease; this can cure disease." For five years he ran over and knocked on all doors, and everybody laughed at him. Then World War II came along, and soldiers were dying of infection. More people died of infection in the war than by gunshots. In the Civil War, more people died from wound infection than anything else. So, here he's got a cure for it. Penicillin completely stopped the spread of bacteria. He was saying, "Wow," and he runs all over excitedly. That's what a spiritual teacher does—so excitedly, and wants to share it. So, the pay that you get is the joy of the sharing. The only difficulty is, you don't have the amount of time that you would like. You'd like to do all the programs, go to all the speaking engagements, talk to everybody that you could, all day long. But you have rent to pay. So I look at it, if something pays the rent and frees your time so that you can spend that time teaching, then you're giving it back to the world. Do you understand what I'm saying? But to store up riches on earth, I think is foolish. Storing up riches on earth is not appealing. So, all the material things no longer have any appeal.

After January of 1965, there was the instant loss of all the things that motivate average people: success, fame, having lots of patients, being well thought of. All those things were meaningless. So, what was the purpose of going to work at all, and returning to the office? It was really compassion for the suffering of patients, and now I had a new dimension. I could see within the psyche of the patient the real source of the illness, and that they were devoid of the recognition, the validation of the true Self within. Because their external was so repulsive, very often, that there was really nobody, even their own mother couldn't love them, see. So, what they needed was somebody that could discern the "Self" with a capital S within and acknowledged its presence. Instantly they felt healed. When you feel acknowledged and gotten and understood, that instant of connection only takes a split second. It can happen anywhere in the world at any time. Instantly, there's a mutual recognition of the truth of who you are. Once that's validated, after that, things don't really matter. Whether you get better in terms of the world or not is sort of irrelevant. The capacity to do that is what propelled the continuation: the joy of one's perfection or expertise, or whatever you call it.

You know, musicians typically live to be very old, and so do humorists and artists. It's not unusual for a symphony conductor to father a child at 92. And 30 years after other people have retired and died already, they're still writing and conducting symphonies. Artists tend to be long-lived, and humorists—they live into their late 90s. So, there's something about humor and art and music that is somehow life-sustaining. That's interesting, isn't it?

When I was young, you worked for the company until you were 65. You got a gold watch, and they had a big retirement party. You then got with your wife in a rec-reational vehicle, toured the United States, came home, and dropped dead in two years. So, everybody retired at 65, had a retirement party, toured the world, and dropped dead at 67, because now you don't have a title, you have no name; there's no reason to continue on.

Depression and Brain Chemistry

One can unravel depression from various viewpoints. Of course, it's seen as hopelessness, lack of self-worth; it's sometimes expressed as anger turned within oneself. So, there's a personal self-evaluation there. We'll skip the karma in the whole story. We'll go to the brain chemistry. You can turn depression on and off by raising and lowering one of the brain's neurotransmitters. Genetically, about a third of mankind is prone to depression. Women are more prone than men. Certain age groups are more prone. You can turn depression on and off by raising and lowering one of the brain's neurotransmitters. So, that's the physiology, the physicality, the genetics of it. The karmic propensity is something else. It comes from self-evaluation; it's really due to the lack of joy in the experience of one's own existence. The answer is, truthfully—aside from the brain chemistry—spiritual. And it resolves only when one surrenders the depression to God and says, "I will be of service, even though I am useless and hateful; but, even as that, I will continue to serve," and the depression will lift itself. It's, to some degree, a narcissistic self-evaluation which the degree of narcissism refuses the judgment of the world. The judgment of the world is that you're a good father and husband, and all that and the other. But the ego, in its sort of megalomania, disputes that and says, on the contrary, "You are wrong, and I am right." So there's a vanity of the ego at the core of it. It's not really "cured" until that narcissistic core of the ego is resolved, surrendered to a higher power. Nothing that you think about yourself is true. It has no validity. Whether you think you're great or you think you're horrible, they're both irrational and somewhat lunatic. If you think you're great, that is a moment of lunacy, and if you think you're awful, that's an equal moment of lunacy. There's no validity in anything the ego says about itself, you know.

What I really try to convey is a grasp of the difference between the linear and the nonlinear, because to know under which bush to look is very helpful. Understand what I'm saying? That's what I'm really trying to say. Too many things say: "Well, we're looking here while you're looking there, 'cause that's where the light is," right? But, the keys were lost over here, right. So we're trying to create an understanding of how to approach that which is really unapproachable from the world of the ego, without ending up in the dead end of many religious rigidities and belief systems. Enlightenment is quite a bit different than being a religionist.

PART II

Radical Subjectivity: The "I" of Self

CHAPTER 7

A Different Paradigm of Reality

When I wrote *Power vs. Force*, 85 percent of the world's population calibrated below 200, 200 being the critical level of integrity. Below 200, everything makes you go weak with kinesiology; above 200 makes you go strong. It differentiates truth from falsehood and various degrees of, really, spiritual energy. You might say the energy field of Divine Love is the most strong at this level and diminishes as you go this way.

God is both immanent and transcendent. Religion has to do with God as transcendent. Spirituality, Enlightenment, the way of Zen and the ancient mystics is through within—the discovery of God immanent, rather than transcendent. You might say the ego is like clouds, and as you remove the clouds, the sun shines forth. Up until recent times, 1,000 calibrates the levels of the great spiritual beings of history. And that has been the limit of human physiology. The human nervous system, until almost now, could only handle up to 1,000—and then with some difficulty; in fact, with great difficulty. And then, as it goes down, you see what happens is, the clouds begin to obscure the sky and therefore, that is what is indicated by the shading. They will try to improve on the chart even further.

So we're starting with a recapitulation, really, of the Map of Consciousness®, because historically that's how it evolved. The work was first published as a Ph.D. dissertation called *Qualitative and Quantitative Analysis and*

Calibration of the Level of Human Consciousness, complete with the null hypothesis, p < 0.001, statistical analysis; and it was sufficiently impressive that, when presented to the faculty who I asked to all vote on it—I presented it during their vacation time, and the dean called them back from their vacation. Would you believe the academic committee came back from their vacation to review the material because they thought it was so remarkable? Actually, it's the $E = mc^2$ of the nonlinear domain, so I guess that caused excitement. I say these things from a jocular viewpoint, you understand.

At 431, you can see one is pretty well on their way to the light. They're pretty much in the light. That's traditionally the level of the intellect, the capacity to reason and think, which is of great benefit. Whatever is of great benefit to get up to here then becomes a block to getting beyond it. So, after struggling your whole life to perfect your intellect, you now find that it is the main obstacle. And we discovered that 4 percent of the world's population goes from 500 up. When you get to 540, the number of people that reach this is 0.4 percent. Zero point four. So we drop from 4 percent to 0.4 percent. The difficulty is that it's very hard to transcend the level 499; 499 is the limit of the intellect. Einstein, Sir Isaac Newton, all the great scientific geniuses, Freud, all calibrated 499. And if you go back to Sir Francis Bacon, all the great scientific intellects throughout history seem to stop at 499. The *Great Books of the Western World* were done in the University of Chicago, I think, back in the '30s. Let's see what their level is . . . "The *Great Books of the Western World* are the greatest philosophic insights in intelligence throughout all of history. I have permission: resist" (True). "It's over 450" (True); "460" (True); "465" (True); "470" (True); "480" (True); "485"

(True); "490" (True); "495" (True); "496" (Not true). The *Great Books of the Western World* calibrate at 496. So, that's the accumulated wisdom of the greatest intellects in all of history. Of course, the *Great Books of the Western World* exclude spirituality. And so, it's as far as philosophy can take you.

Radical Subjectivity: What Is It?

So, we're talking about radical subjectivity. Spirituality has to do with discovering a different paradigm of reality. Science, the world up to 499, the Newtonian paradigm, has to do with form. It has to do with content. Spirituality has to do with context and not content, and it is a different paradigm. Now, the difficulty in society is, society is in the linear paradigm. In society, the Newtonian paradigm is what's real. That is traditional science. Science is in the low . . . well, in the 400s; 420 to 425 and up. Medicine is maybe around 430. Psychiatry is maybe five points higher, but it is still within the linear paradigm, which as we know from our own spiritual research and personal experience is a very limited paradigm of reality.

The spiritual dimension has to do with context. And it is, first of all, unlimited; it is nonlinear, and it is touched by advanced theoretical physics, which realizes that no further advance can be made in understanding the reality of the universe without understanding the nature of consciousness itself—which accounts for the conferences on science and consciousness which have occurred. And I've spoken at a few in Tucson [and] in New Mexico. They had a few of them, maybe three in a row at the University of Arizona, but they have stopped; they probably blew their wires out—because there's quite a war, ideologic war, between traditional science and advanced consciousness. And traditional sides, to some degree, feel greatly threatened by the nonlinear domain, that there is a dimension beyond the comprehension of the intellect.

Therefore, there is the linear domain. That is the realm of the ego. It is the traditional world of our civilization. Beyond that is the nonlinear domain: the nonlinear, which is approached via science and a form of chaos theory. Chaos theory begins to sense that there's something beyond that which is countable, calculable, measurable, that can be weighed, identified and photographed; that there is another reality. And that is just where it's pushing forward to try to comprehend the nonlinear domain.

Spirituality is the nonlinear domain which creates context. Science and linear domain create content. But meaning doesn't come out of content. Meaning comes out of context. Consequently, science is unable to grasp the "meaning" of anything, which is a bit of a limitation. When atomic reaction occurs—"What'll I do with it? Should I blow up the world or . . . create energy, or what?"

The difficulty, then, is that context is what creates meaning, significance. All of human life is lived from the nonlinear domain. Although we handle an object here in the linear, it's the nonlinear that gives it significance. It gives it meaning.

Human life, then, is lived subjectively as the experiential presence of consciousness itself as it registers the linear domain—it's not the linear domain, but what it means to you. What is a million dollars? It's what it means to you. If I stack a million dollars here, it's just a bunch of paper; it's a nuisance. It'd be right in the way, wouldn't it? I'd be moving the million dollars all the time. No, it's what it means to us, what it means to us. So, the human is run by significance and meaning, which is in the nonlinear domain. Significance and meaning are conveyed by a flick of the eyebrow. You're out someplace in public, and your father flicks his eyebrow—*wham*! That totally changed your life right that instant—nothing was said. You *get* the meaning of that: "Keep that up and you're gonna hear about it when you get home, young man." So, the significance, then—meaning, value, all the things that we live for, and motivate all of life—are all in the nonlinear domain.

They may find expression in the linear domain. A new Mercedes Benz is in the linear domain, but it's what it *means* to you.

So, reality, then, is what we have agreed reality is: the linear. But the linear is always subjectively experienced by consciousness, which is in the nonlinear. Therefore, the radical materialist is up against the absurdity that if only an objective, scientifically measurable kind of a world is objective and true and verifiable, then by what right does he say so? Because that is a subjective conclusion there. So the objective world doesn't even exist except as is experienced subjectively. It is the subjective reality that we're talking about in spiritual evolution. In the book I'm working on now, I try to track the evolution of consciousness throughout all of time—throughout the universe, expressing itself as this universe, this planet, the evolution of life on this planet, from the beginning up to the present time. That takes a couple of pages already. Actually, all such things are simple when you see them. So, when you see them, they are all quite simple.

The Mystic

The mystic, then . . . the mystic is one who realizes the Presence of God as the Unmanifest becoming manifest as consciousness, awareness, and the radical subjectivity of the sense of "I." Therefore, the book I'm finishing now is just called *The Eye of the I*. *The Eye of the I* is coming, really, through the third eye of the Buddhic body, in a way, but it's preparing the way. The first one, the Ph.D. thesis, was a scientific basis I thought most comprehensible by the academic world. And then pushed it a little bit over to the nonlinear and used something safe and familiar to the intellect, the academic intellect—and that was that graph, and we used logarithms and things that people are comfortable with. And then we moved on to *The Eye of the I*, which was the evolution of that to its higher significance and dimensions, and I hope to conclude it with the book I'm just finishing now. What we're tracking, then, is subjective experience.

The subjective experience has to do with physicality, and it really emanates from the animal domain. When you track, "What is the ego, anyway? Is it something evil? Is it something to be fought? Something to be ashamed of? Conquered?" you hear all kinds of approaches to the ego. It's the screaming maniac that you have to quell, et cetera—the wild ox of the Zen ox-herding pictures. It arises—if you track it back as to its etiology—its origin is really within the animal domain. It's really within the animal domain. You won't find anything in your ego that you can't see at the nearest Monkey Island. If you go to the zoo and watch Monkey Island, there's your ego, right there. They're grasping, they're challenging each other, they're baring their teeth. They're trying to grab each other and mate right on the spot and fight off all the females fighting for the male, the males fighting for the females. You see this alpha male and female dominance. And you see people looking for favoritism; you see people codependent with each other and "Love me 'because I love you.'" You see all of human pathology exhibited there—paranoia, possessiveness, territoriality. All you see is today's headline. I didn't see this morning's headline, but I'm sure it's right from the latest review from Monkey Island.

So if you look at the ego, all we see is really the dominance of the animal within us. Of course, the animal, the animal within us, is still present anatomically as the old animal brain. So, being a human being is a very difficult thing. If I were Saint Peter, I'd say, "Are you human?" "Yeah." "You pass." Anybody who survives a total life as a human being is in a terrible conflict from the instant you're here. Why? Because you have an animal body. It's made of meat and bones and the same thing as a cow or a horse. Within the brain you have atavistic drives built into your brain. The basic nuclei in the brain are built into survival, hating rivals. Here you have an animal body, you have the remnants of the old reptilian—not only the animal, but reptilian brain. And then, superimposed, the mammalian brain, and then lastly, the cerebral cortex in the frontal region: the cerebral cortex, which is a very late arrival in the human scene—a couple hundred thousand years, which is practically no time at all. Therefore, it's helpful to realize we're a primitive race. My view of mankind is that it is a very primitive race, barely out of the animal stage.

Why can we say that? Well, we see that 87 percent of the people are not out of the animal stage yet, you know? The human, the light of humanness dimly dawns on some people, but it's a late arrival. It's only in late 1986 or so that the consciousness level of mankind jumped from 190 to 207. In other words, like yesterday. Well. Consciousness level 200 here is the difference between that which is destructive to life, negative to life, and that which is spiritually aware. So you don't really see the beginning of Love until 200. Love doesn't count in the world of survival. On the battlefield, forget it; and you're selling used cars, forget it. A friend of mine who was here last time sells used cars. I mean, the idea has to do with survival.

The Evolution of Consciousness

All right. So, this evolution of consciousness, then, which evolved in the beginning: Genesis makes you go strong. In the beginning, out of the non-form, non-anythingness, arose light. Light, then, was the energy of the Unmanifest becoming manifest. The first sign of any Divinity in the universe, as far as we know, is light. Let's see if that's so. "The first emanation of God as manifest was as light: resist" (True). So, Genesis makes you go strong. Genesis . . . there's only three books of the Old Testament that make you go strong. Genesis is one of them. Proverbs is another, and Psalms is another. The rest of them make you go weak and seem to come out of sort of a primitive religion—a primitive religion in which the view of God is an anthropomorphic projection from the unconscious of all that is negative and feared.

The evolution of consciousness, then, takes us through. This energy is coming up through the animal kingdom. There's a bifurcation in the animal kingdom, a very strange one. If we go back to the lowest forms of life, we find that there is no concern for others. It's rapacious and it lives by virtue of destroying the life of another. This reaches its epitome during the age of the dinosaur. The dinosaur was probably the epitome of that energy when it reigned upon the earth, rapacious with no concern for anything except its own greedy survival. The maternal instinct had not arisen as yet. The dinosaur laid an egg and wished it well. Good luck.

But then there arose a parallel line of evolution, the warm-blooded herbivore. The herbivore does not kill anything in order to eat. In fact, the herbivore supports life. The green grass grows, the herbivore eats it. It represents combining oxygen and chlorophyll. And then refertilizes the earth, which makes for more grass, so the herbivore doesn't have to kill anything or anybody in order to survive. So, you have that which survives only by killing, and that which survives without killing.

And the evolution of Love, as I'm tracking the evolution of consciousness, doesn't begin until it arises on the planet as maternal love. The mother's caring for the infant is the first dawning of Love on the planet. Until that, until mammalian love or the bird's mother caring for the egg, Love didn't really exist. Does a dinosaur love another dinosaur? Not likely.

You might say the appearance of spiritual energy, then, was in the form of the mother, and much later, between man and woman. Romantic love is a very recent development. It's only a few hundred years old. The upper classes didn't pay any attention to love; you married for what was good for the family, and then you found love elsewhere. Men and women, until very recent times, spent very little time with each other. The man was out hunting and fishing and brawling and doing unmentionable things. And the woman was home taking care of domestic issues. They spent very little time. There was very little companionship between man and woman. So, romantic love is really quite recent—really, in the late feudal period. The idea of romance between man and woman is a pretty modern kind of a thing. So, even romantic love is very recent on the planet. One would assume it was always there, but if you look back through history, you realize it was relatively rare.

At 431, where we are today, we're looking at God as wisdom; meaningful; He's approachable by reason; we're capable of understanding Him; and the mind at this point is capable of abstraction. Well, at the lower levels, the mind is very concrete. It's not capable of abstraction. As people evolve and reason begins to really take hold, they hear a spiritual truth, and a certain percentage becomes attracted to it. That starts the spiritual quest, either through an emotional hitting bottom or by the sheer advance of consciousness and its evolution as it is expressed as reason. So, 431 is a very high level. It surpasses most of mankind. Any guy who's watching the TV news will tell you that. The world is so stupid. That's what a guy is supposed to say to his wife: "God, it's so stupid!" He's all upset about politics, and she's not interested in politics.

So, radical subjectivity, then, is the very essence of experiencing the Presence of God as that which says "I": that which allows you to be aware of your own existence, is at all times present, never absent. It's the first thing you become aware of when you wake up in the morning. The first thing that happens before thinkingness even starts is the awareness of existence. There's an awareness, as you wake up, that one exists. You don't even have a name yet. If I catch you at the very first instant you open your eyes and say, "What's your name?" "Give me a second while I wake up. Give me a second." "Are you a man or a woman?" "Go ahead, give me a second until I wake up." "Are you an American or European, or what are you?" "Give me a second to wake up." So, consciousness is there before even content. Consciousness awakens, then, with the awareness of existence. That which allows you to say "I" is presumed, as you wake up, to be the personal "I." Because reality seems to have to do with form and facts and physicality, one presumes that knowing that I am, that I exist, being aware, the sense of "I," is coming from a personal "I." And that's the only illusion we have to jump.

The sense of "I" is not coming from a personal "I" at all. It's coming from an impersonal "I." Consciousness is an impersonal quality. The consciousness which arises as you awaken is not personal at all. You have it *focused* on the personal, but its essence is not personal; it is because of the Infinite "I," that which is not different than Divinity, reality, truth, all the things it's been called throughout the ages. It illuminates the awareness that shines forth as the awareness of your own existence, but its source is the Infinite "I."

That which knows that you're here this second is not the personal "I," because if we ablate the personal "I," you will still be aware that one's quality is that of existence. It was that dilemma that confronted me at age three. People say, "We'd like to hear personal stories." The personal story is actually irrelevant, but it gives an example of what we're talking about.

In this lifetime, at age three, out of complete oblivion and nothingness, suddenly there was a shock. This thing here was sitting in a little wagon, and I realized I exist. It was the awareness of existence with extreme clarity and extremely shocking intensity; nor was I pleased with it. There was a shocking awareness of existence. Instantly arose a fear. If I had come into existence, then hypothetically it might have been that I might *not* have come into existence. So, it was really the awareness of existence as

"beingness," "I am–ness." At three, there was no verbalization about any of this, but it was a complete understanding of it, let me tell you. And it really set the theme for this
lifetime for many years to come. That dilemma of reality
as "existence versus nonexistence" is extremely abstract
and extremely high level. It's a spiritual paradox you don't
have to solve until you get to level 890 or something,
which was difficult to handle, therefore, at age three.

But the dilemma of existence versus nonexistence was
like a silent paradox that hung out in the back of my mind
in the lifelong pursuit of identifying the radical truth of
the Self and who you are. And it wasn't verbalized again
for many years, but there was the paradox of existence versus nonexistence.

The beautiful thing about realizing the truth of who
you are—the truth of who you are is not different than
that which subjectively is conscious of your existence.
Nothing needs to be said about it. It doesn't have to be
searched for. You don't have to study to find it. It's more
an intuitive awareness that sort of dawns on you that that
is the ultimate reality you've been searching for. That
ultimate reality is timeless; and as one becomes aware of
it, one realizes that that which you really are has always
existed. You'll always exist, because it is beyond existence
versus nonexistence. It is beyond time. It is beyond form.
It is the substrate out of which all experiencing arises and
that solves all the riddles.

Now, religion says such an awareness is not possible
until after you're dead and in heaven or someplace. So
religion looks at God as transcendent. The transcendent
God shows up in Genesis, creates the universe, promptly
disappears, and goes in heaven—moves to heaven—and
you don't get any chance to meet Him until after you're

dead, if you've been good. There is that horrible moment called Judgment Day, though. Uh-oh! God rolls the dice, says, "Good luck, you're on your own." Then He hangs out in heaven, waiting for you with a big stick. And, if you didn't do so well—*whacko*! Into the boiling cauldron—out of which He gets great glee, by the way. He *loves* to see people *suffer*. Anyway, He picks the good and the bad, or He picks 144,000.

So, that is the God who is transcendent; to be feared; projected somewhere, elsewhere in time and space; because heaven is up there and you're down here. Well, if you're down here and heaven and God is up there, the chances are not too good you're going to run into Him at Walmart.

Traditional religion, then, is a denial of the reality of the truth of yourself. It is in great contrast to the mystic. Religion, therefore, is extremely limited as compared to spirituality. So, we differentiate between religion and spirituality: a very delicate but important difference to be made. The signers of the Constitution understood it perfectly. The Constitution of the United States calibrates at over 700. That is spiritual brilliance. That's the level of the sage, the genius. It clearly differentiates spiritual freedom from the establishment of religion and clearly saw that, if anything, religion is an enemy of spiritual freedom. Of course, coming out of England, and Protestant and Catholic conflicts over the years, et cetera, they were highly conscious of that. But I don't think it came out of their historical experience. It came out of, really, a spiritual inspiration because the signers of the Declaration of Independence, et cetera, all calibrate in the high 500s. They were extremely gifted men, and we are very, very fortunate. The Constitution of the United States calibrates higher than the constitution of any [other] country on the planet. It guarantees spiritual freedom, and it does so by prohibiting religion from becoming established, and simultaneously it does not prohibit religion. So, it was extremely brilliant. Very few people today really comprehend the difference between spiritual and religious.

So religion becomes, over time, an institution which has its upside and its downside. In another book we're doing right now, we calibrate the level of truth for all the world's great religions, and you can track it down through time. You can track it down from the time of its origination, down through the centuries and down through the Council of Trent, the Council of Nicaea, all the various things—and see what happened to all the various world's religions.

Traditionally, the mystic has been at odds with traditional religion. In fact, some religions condemn the mystic, and historically, mystics were burned at the stake and declared heretics—excommunicated and put in strange places. In some world's religions, actually, the subjective reality of the mystic is declared to be formally heresy. To experience the Presence of God within is actually forbidden in Islam, for instance. So the Christian mystic didn't do too well either.

The only place the mystic has really prospered in history has been in areas of India, where their tradition of the mystic is traditional. The Vedas explain the realization of the Presence of God as Self, for some thousands of years. All those, by the way, do calibrate at 1,000, as does the Buddha, who cleverly got himself born in India so that he didn't get crucified for his teachings. Had he been born elsewhere, he would not have fared as well. But there was already a friendly knowledge of spiritual truth in that part of the world of great antiquity. So, what he taught was not at great odds with their tradition. The lands that are favorable to Buddhism are today the most favorable to the mystic. When we speak in Korea, let's say, or the Orient, you know, they come by the thousands from all over the country, because all we are saying is that we have sort of demonstrated in a scientific, verifiable way what their culture has held to be the truth for thousands of years.

The prosperity of a religion or a spiritual teaching depends considerably, then, on context. On context, not just on content. The religionist tends to emphasize *content* and declare holy wars based on content, thereby negating the context. But it is the context out of which their spiritual teaching is true. Without context, what they're babbling is nonsense. Any mental hospital is full of religious people that can babble all kinds of religious stuff. It's the context that gives the spiritual teaching any kind of validity because *God is the ultimate context*. That which is God derives its infinite power by the fact that Divinity is infinite context. Out of infinite context comes infinite power. So, religion which negates context has just negated its own validity.

Spiritual seekers are made up considerably by people who've had a variety of religious backgrounds. And many have ridden it as far as it can go and then wanna know: "Where do we go from here?" Some people have had subjective spiritual experiences which are quite powerful. In this lifetime, such things occurred. At age 12 or 14, a near-death experience which was transformative totally eliminated the fear of death for the rest of my life. And in the late 30s, suddenly, all that the mind had considered "myself" in reality completely disappeared and was replaced by an infinite context, which was the presence which swept away all thought.

So, those kinds of severe spiritual experiences, then, account for some of us being here. Other people become interested in spiritual work because they have a variety of illnesses. And they've heard that, through spiritual investigation, every illness known to mankind has been known to become healed and resolved, and I myself have witnessed it. It is true that with intense spiritual work, a certain percentage of physical illnesses will remit or totally cure. In some cases they will not, but to a spiritually evolved person, it no longer matters whether it does or it doesn't. So, the fallacy of criticizing that spiritual work did not lead to the healing of something means that the person did not evolve enough.

You follow *A Course in Miracles*, let's say, with great intensity—or even AA, even the 12 Steps—you take the third step of the 12 Steps with great intensity; you finally reach a state whether the physicality survives or not is totally irrelevant. Because when you totally surrender your will to God, the craving for continued physicality disappears. And whether this physicality survives or not is, frankly, of no interest whatsoever. So, a person who intensely does spiritual work will either recover from the physical illness or they will reach such an advanced state of consciousness that whether the body survives or not is really not of any particular interest. They will even reach a point where if they left soon, that would be fine. So, spiritual endeavor, then, does handle any and all physical illnesses.

Anybody who has been around in any of the consciousness teachings that are prevalent—*A Course in Miracles* is one I was familiar with—we saw people with every illness on the face of the earth go into remission or recover. And that started these Attitudinal Healing centers which were based on that group: a spiritual approach to chronic and incurable illnesses. Jerry Jampolsky started one out in Tiburon [California]. He wrote *Love Is Letting Go of Fear*. Jampolsky brought his whole staff back east, where I had a big clinic. We started the second Attitudinal Healing center in New York. And there we did also see every kind of illness known to mankind remit. And this particular body, which was afflicted with all kinds of disasters in my 30s, slowly remitted from a whole lot of these disasters, including the ability to see.

When I grew up, I had thick glasses and I was what you call nowadays a nerd—no doubt. While everybody played stickball, I sat there reading Plato. It does sound kind of nerdy when I look at it now. I liked Aristophanes and Plato and Aristotle, and those are my heroes. With thick bifocals on, you can't play baseball too well, because it hits you in the nose before you see it. You're too small and skinny to play football. I tried the swimming team, and they said, "You're way too short." So Plato was my pal. But anyway, after this transformation of consciousness, many ailments healed themselves. And I still wore thick trifocals then. While in *A Course in Miracles* class, somebody said, "Why do you still wear them?" And I thought, *Huh, I never thought of that as a belief system*. I always thought, being a physician in training and being a physician, that nearsightedness and astigmatism and all those things were physical, due to faulty construction of the eyeball and the lens, et cetera. So I never thought of it as an illness due to a belief system. I put the glasses away in my pocket and never took them out again.

So then I had to drive blind for six weeks. Happily, I wasn't living in New York City anymore. But it was interesting because what I needed to see, I could see. See, when you surrender every instant, when you stop trying to control or change every instant as it arises—as the wave of the instant arises—you surrender it as it arises; so you begin riding the crest of the instant of "now." And as you do that—I would always be able to see just what I needed to see: the pedestrian right before I ran over him, so I missed him; the stop sign turning red, et cetera. Driving around Sedona, I can remember driving around the edge of the cliff and I could just see the edge of the cliff, so I was surrendering fear all the time. And I would just see the edge of the cliff as I needed to see it. I'd go to make a left turn in the dark and the rain, and all of a sudden, I would see the curb that I was supposed to see, because the headlights of some car would mysteriously arrive from someplace and illuminate the curb, and I'd make it. If you look at it through the intellect, it's hairy, but—anyway, for six weeks I surrendered my survival to the Presence of God. The Infinite Presence guided everything, which it has since 1965.

It's Because of the Self That You Survive, Not the Ego

The ego sells you the illusion that it's because of the ego that you survive, but actually it's because of the Self with a capital *S* that you survive. It certainly was not the ego keeping me alive. Anyway, I thought, *Well, I guess you'll never get to see anything again.* I mean, I couldn't see this crowd here, in a way. I couldn't see the table. I can't see anything close, and I can't see anything far. If you can't see either close or far, then you can't see anything, can you? I knew if it was light or dark. So, one day I was standing in the kitchen of a friend, and—I think it was *A Course in Miracles* class, in fact. We were standing in the kitchen, the friend, talking about this, that, or the other thing, and suddenly, with no warning, everything became clearly visible. I looked at the calendar across the room. I could read the calendar—January, February, March, April . . . So, even vision returned with great clarity. And a number of people who've heard the story tried it and had the same experience. And they all said it took about six weeks. Anyway, that's the six-week program, folks—anybody who's willing to drive in traffic without knowing where you're going until the last instant, if your nerves can take it.

As we progress spiritually, various peculiar phenomena do occur. There are physiologic changes that happen, and they differ depending where you are along the path. Some are exquisite. Some are beyond description. There's also various psychic, paranormal—the so-called Siddhis that arise, which spiritual debunkers like to attack. There's also paranormal kinds of things arise. There's exquisitely pleasurable sensations. Then, as you get higher and higher, at least in this particular case, there's extremely awful kinds of pain and you get wracked by all kinds of discomforts. So, we'll try to recontextualize all these things. The physiology of the nervous system literally changes as you advance spiritually. There are shifts in the brain's neurotransmitters. There is a shift from adrenaline to endorphins as a predominant motif, neurochemically speaking. There's a diminishing in, and finally the elimination of, the startle reflex. As a shot goes off behind me, I don't react at all. When I say "by me," I'm talking about this body. If a shot goes off, it's a passing notice, but there's no sense of alarm. That disappeared after the near-death experience.

In World War II, there was no fear of death either. We'd be facing imminent, certain death, and I felt high. People were throwing up on the deck, and I felt exhilarated. I was in a state of happiness. I guess I thought I was soon to be with God. So there's a difference in emotional reactions, and there are really profound changes throughout the human body. And I think the healing process which many people come to Sedona, seeking healing for various things, which we explained in the last lecture and previous ones. The energy field of Love, to choose Love, then tends to favor a healing and a healthiness of the entire acupuncture system and a strengthening of the immune system. I think any illness, if you become interested in intense spiritual work—and by intense, I mean intense—you can transcend the level at which that illness will remit.

CHAPTER 8

Understanding Karmic Influences

There are also karmic influences that may prevail. There are many times when karmic deterrents to healing become transcended and the person goes into remission. There are certain serious karmic limitations, perhaps, that preclude the absolute healing of certain conditions, you see. So, each and every case is researched; that's why we find kinesiology very fun and useful. We find it's very useful in karmic research, because some trait or some persistence in your life that's not explicable by logic, with a few questions, you can find out where that originated, and sometimes you can even recall it. It wasn't this lifetime—no, it wasn't this lifetime. But you do remember it.

I know why I don't get along with horses. I just don't get on with horses. I also remember where that all started. Anyway, let's see if we've transcended that one with horses or not. "We have transcended that one with horses: resist" (True). Yes, we did. I was very mean to horses, and they also were very mean to me, and we just didn't get along for a lot of lifetimes. In fact, that might have even remitted this week, yes. There was a horse out in the corral and crying, crying, crying. All the other horses had gone out on the trail, and this horse just cried and cried and was just carrying on. And I couldn't stand it. So I was at the girls' ranch where I am the chief of staff there. They have 50 adolescent girls. I said, "I have to take care of this."

I couldn't stand this horse crying, obviously with emotional pain and acute separation anxiety. So, I stopped everything to go out and comfort this horse and began talking to that horse, who realized that compassion was paying attention to it—the horse got that. It didn't heal the horse, but I think the horse did get a message. But it could be where that remitted, anyway.

The Muscle-Testing Technique

Now let's talk about kinesiology. We don't teach kinesiology. We explain how to do it, and then it's up to you. It's like learning how to ride a bicycle. I can't really run bicycle-riding classes. But we do give you references where you can go. People ask us . . . we have a sheet that gives references on kinesiology. Jerry Teplitz, I just happen to be familiar with. He puts out a whole course called Switched-On Living which demonstrates it in spades. Also, it's not a technique that everyone can do, but you can find people who are able to do it, and if you have a distinct question—should you kill yourself or not, or go to a movie—you can ask them. That's one of my favorite quotes: "I couldn't decide whether to go to a movie this afternoon or commit suicide."

When two people are calibrating a thing or event, why do they get different answers? This is a relative scale. If you really are serious about it, first of all, you don't have to calibrate anything; I've already done it for you. But if you're going to be do-it-yourself-ish, you have to do it yourself. You can use the single-ring technique. If it's an important question, we suggest you find a partner you can work with. For some people it comes very rapidly. When I first saw it, I "got" how to do it in an instant. It's why I tend to be impatient with people that take weeks to get what I could see in one instant. So I'm not a great teacher of it. Teplitz has Switched-On Living. There's a book by a nurse that's very good. If you call or write our office, we have references on kinesiology. John Diamond's book *Your Body Doesn't Lie* is about as good a description of the technique as you will find anywhere, and it has illustrations. Another book [by Diamond] that is also out is *Behavioral Kinesiology*. John Diamond, M.D.'s *Your Body Doesn't Lie* is a very good reference. And Jerry Teplitz has an elaboration of it with videos and audios. So that's a good way to learn it.

To really define it for yourself, you have to say, "in reference to this scale of consciousness." You can use any scale. You can make up your own scale. But "in reference to this scale of consciousness": you have to give conscious reference to it. I used to say, "On a scale of consciousness from 1 to 1,000, where 200 is Integrity and 500 is Love," or "where 200 is Integrity and 600 is Enlightenment," on that scale of consciousness, then: "The answer to this question is so-and-so." You understand? It's an arbitrary scale. We could have made it from 1 to 100; we could have made it from 0 to .1, and you could have .001, .0001— you see. Anyway, this turned out to be logarithmically so, because I asked, "Is this numeric?" It said, "No, it's logarithmic." All right. So it's a logarithmic scale. If you want accuracy, then you have to say: "In reference to this scale, where 200 is Integrity and 600 is Enlightenment, this dog calibrates at so-and-so." I've already told you in previous lectures that the dog's wagging tail calibrates at 500. And so does a cat's purr. And Koko—you know, the gorilla— calibrates over 200. And there's a famous gray parrot, out of the University of Arizona, that can count and tell colors. He knows which is gray and he knows which is cork.

He calibrates over 200. So you're safer with the gorilla, Koko, than you are with 78 percent of the people on the planet, who'll steal your wallet while they're doing kinesiology with you.

What Is a Genuine Mystic?

What percentage of genuine mystics are alive in the world today? What is a genuine mystic? "A genuine mystic is— they mean by this somebody who calibrates over 600: resist" (True). Okay. What percent are alive in the world today? We can't get percentage, because it's less than 0.01 or something like that. We can get the number, though. "The number of people on the planet today who calibrate over 600 is over 30" (True); "32" (Not true). It's between 30 and 32. Let's see; where's that other scale we had up here? These were revised periodically because these changed between 1995 and the year 2001. Let's do the rest. "The number of people 700 is more than six" (True); "More than eight" (Not true); "More than seven" (True); "More than eight" (Not true). "The number over 800 is more than two" (True); "Three" (Not true). "The number over 900 is more than two" (True). "The number over 980 is more than one" (True); "Two." (Not true). One over 980.

Surrendering the Ego to God

Now, how does one go about surrendering the ego to God? Can intention alone change your consciousness? Yes. It's intention that motivates the whole spiritual effort. It's one's intention that sets the context, and then everything else falls within that context. You see, the mind will automatically prioritize everything. If your most intense intention is to reach the conscious experience of the Presence of God, then everything gets subsumed under that. The mind then automatically discards things that would be extraneous.

I can remember going through medical school. I put my way through college and medical school. The financial demand of getting through medical school and the intellectual demand of endless hours of study took priority over everything. There was no time to read novels; there was no time to go to movies. Every dollar had to count, so that prioritized everything. I was a cabdriver, as my wife well knows, and every second counted. Every second was money. When the light turned green and the oncoming traffic—if they didn't instantly jump it, I had made my left already. The intention, then, is very determinative.

How Do You Surrender the Ego to God?

The books I'm writing have to do with understanding the mechanisms of the ego. Before, we talked about positionality. Then we talked about how the ego arose as survival mechanism in the animal world. It then became elaborated by the intellect. The intellect now becomes the instrument of the animal instinct. It's still up to the same thing; it's just more sophisticated. To be top dog now means the brand of car you drive and its year, or one's position or one's title or one's income, or the store you bought your clothes, or the style. So the intellect has merely become the servant of the animal and expresses itself in more sophisticated ways. It's still up to being the king of the hill and being the alpha male or the alpha female, et cetera. If you see that the ego arose, it's not different than the animal, and its motivations are not different than the animal, then you can stop feeling guilt about it and stop making it wrong.

There are many spiritual teachings that tend to make the ego wrong and label all its on-going-ness as sin. Sin is just the persistence of the animal to give in to biologic drives, at the price of a more evolved kind of human love. Then it gets labeled "sin." So, sin would be that which is still innate to the animal kingdom, and by being human, it is now expected that you will transcend it and not be *dominated* by the animal drive. It doesn't mean that you don't have the animal drive, but it means you won't be dominated by it.

The reason I tracked the origin of consciousness as it evolved throughout all of evolution is to disassemble the guilt-and-shame mechanism which precludes many people from serious spiritual or religious endeavor. In the 12-Step groups, many people buck at the fourth step. The fourth step is a "fearless, searching, moral inventory." A lot of people will go to the third step, but when they get to the fourth step, they don't want to go to AA anymore because they're faced with what looks to them an ominous guilt trip. Well. How can you look at the downside of the ego without succumbing to guilt and shame and anger, et cetera? If you realize it is just the persistence of the animal, you can get off moralizing about it. And if you can get off moralizing about it, you can avoid spiritual guilt. If you've listened to enough confessions, you'll realize that everybody's ego is the same. The next penitent in the booth is just going to tell you the same thing the last 10 thousand told you. "I lied to my mother." "I cheated on my wife." "I'm lusting after my secretary." "I took pens home from the office." "I stole paper clips." I mean, what does the ego do? It's acquisitive, huh? And it's carnal. And it's lascivious and libidinous, and it gets hooked on those things. So the difficulty with addiction is, it gets hooked on it.

So, the first thing we do is try to grasp the totality of the ego, and the best way is to contextualize how it evolved throughout all of history, which is what I'm doing in this current book. The reason I disagree with the textbook—I like *A Course in Miracles*; I think it's a great thing. I mean, it just blows you out when you read the sentence, "My thoughts don't mean anything." Whoa! Somebody with a college education—"*my thoughts don't mean anything?*" I drove a cab all those years to polish up my thoughts, and now you tell me they don't mean anything. Well, because spiritually motivated people are generally in the 400s, I like *A Course in Miracles* because it tends to disassemble the ego as the great thing at which we genuflect. I mean, "My thoughts don't mean anything"; that's my favorite from *A Course in Miracles*. But I don't like the textbook, because the textbook, I think, was sourced from a somewhat different source than the workbook. It tends to polarize one with the ego and pictures the ego as one's enemy, an evil enemy. The animal isn't evil; it's just animal.

The willingness to surrender the lesser for the greater is all that's required: the willingness to question the validity of anything below 200. Let's say you hate somebody, and that hate is "justified." In fact, as a matter of fact, you don't have to go over and over the fact that it's justified; you should grant the ego its wish right in the beginning and say, "Yes, it is justified." It *is* justified. He ran off with your wife, ruined your business, burned down your house, and you're pissed at him, right. That's that old joke: The guy standing on the street corner, and his wife has run off, his house has burned down, he's been fired, and he says, "I don't know, God, why me?" And he hears this voice coming out of the heavens: "I don't know, George, there's just something about you pisses me off." Nothing like bad karma to turn a guy into an atheist, huh?

So, how can the ego be surrendered to God? First is to become acquainted with what is the ego. It's a persistence of the animal instinct, but now elaborated through mind, the intellect, and given authenticity by the mutual agreement of society. For many years I ignored current events. I didn't read a newspaper or listen to radio for years and years. Somebody did a make-wrong about it, and I bought it. I let go of the make-wrong about paying attention to the world. That make-wrong is a misinterpretation of the calibrated level of 700, where, let's say, Ramana Maharshi says, "There is no point in trying to change the world, because the world that you see doesn't exist," which is true within a certain context. Within another context, the world is the drama of the ego. I find it fascinating, because what you see is every ego mechanism played out on a grand stage. So if you want to understand your ego, what you try to do is comprehend what goes on in the world and see it in terms of the ego, and you then understand yourself. And you understand the fallacy of the many positions that pertain and are popularized in society—you see right through the fallacy in a way that is expressible through languaging. From the nonlinear domain, you see the idiocy of it. You don't see it as idiocy, but you see beyond it; but you can't explain it. It takes years to learn how to relanguage things in a fluent way to explain that which is obvious so that it makes sense to the intellect.

Being a student of the world, then, you're really a student of the ego. Letting go wanting to change it in the world comes about as a willingness to letting it go within yourself and vice versa. Forgiving the world and forgiving yourself are one and the same thing because the world is just a projection of the ego. You might say, "Well, it's not my ego." Well, it's the collective ego. So you might as well take on the collective ego and do everybody a favor, you know. All the people who haven't gotten around to surrendering their ego, you surrender it for them, and they get jacks for openers—they get into heaven right off the bat. You did it for them. Well, we say that in a jocular fashion, but that's a fact: that every step you take forward spiritually benefits all of mankind.

One person that you forgive already affects the consciousness level of all of mankind. "That's so: resist" (True). "Therefore, everyone is a savior, potential savior: resist" (True). Everyone is a potential savior. Each and every one of us, as we forgive that one person that we hated—we could chop them in small pieces and flush them, because they deserve it. You can't pretend they didn't deserve it, and you can't pretend they didn't do it. It's a fact they did, and they probably do deserve it. But despite that, you still forgive them. That's where the jump is. All right. That comes out of the willingness.

The intention, then, to make these moves comes about from—first of all, it comes about through the heart. I usually don't talk about the heart, because it makes things very short. When you bring up the heart—good-bye. I sit on the heart. I also have to sit on the mind, but the mind is easier to sit on than the heart. To keep the mind functioning in languaging comprehensible to the world took a great deal of effort; it took me many years. The willingness to make these steps comes from the heart. It's because of the innate Love of God you're willing to surrender the hatred. You understand? You don't do it because you intellectually understand that it's a necessary step to reach Enlightenment. The willingness to surrender everything to God, including one's justified hatreds, is strong enough that it brings you to the willingness to surrender them. The willingness to surrender all to God is the all-fire in the middle of it all. It allows you to walk into a hail of bullets—literally to walk into a hail of bullets. "For Thee, O God, I do die with joy." And you walk right into the bullets, and you go into ecstasy. The minute you leave the body—ecstasy! Having done it and remembering it, when done for the Love of God, the immediate experience as you go out of body is ecstasy. You know that you have passed a great barrier and that many have not. One of the great values of war is that it does allow those below 200 to cross over 200. Because when you face death for the belief in a higher good, even if it's for the good of mankind or for the Love of God, then you pass a certain level that those who have not done it cannot pass. So, in a way, war is an opportunity for which many young men seek to reach that level, because you actually have to face literal death to do it. You can't just do it in your imagination. That's one of the side benefits of war, not that I recommend this as the best way possible. But it beats hari-kari, I tell you, because hari-kari was not too great either.

The willingness to surrender one's all: that, as I've said in previous lectures, is the integrity of the kamikaze pilot and a lot of these Islamic zealots; when you calibrate 'em, they actually, literally believe they are doing it for God; and as such, they are over 200. They may be in error, but those who manipulate such people, on the other hand, calibrate at 70. When they get there and find there are 72 virgins, what they don't know is they're over 900 years old. That's the part the guru doesn't tell them.

So, spiritual integrity: spiritual integrity means one does what one does out of the innate love for God. Now, that love for God may not swell up as an outpouringness of emotion. It can be a profound commitment, out of the willingness. So, ascending the ladder, if you want to call it the ladder, then, is based on willingness. The willingness to surrender anything because it stands in the way of your experiencing the Presence of God. So it comes out of a profound commitment and not an emotionality. Emotionality is a substitute for what is really a greater insight. The greater insight is the intuitive understanding of the essence of your own existence and the willingness then to commit to a greater understanding of that reality. Willing to surrender everything to God is the machinery behind all this.

Now, as you take the nature of the ego apart, the work becomes more specific. We've said, religion is one thing; enlightenment is another. Jesus Christ died for the salvation of the world. The Buddha taught enlightenment. Christ taught the way to heaven. There is only one quote we still have, and that is, "Heaven is within you": that God is both transcendent and immanent. But the stress of Christianity is primarily on God as transcendent. Although it is the way of the heart, the Buddha is aimed in a different direction: the realization of the Presence of God as the Buddha nature, as the Reality of the Self. That branch of Buddhism called "Lotus Land" coincides with Christianity, in which the Buddha of the Lotus Land is the Savior.

The aim of Christianity is to reach 540. The ultimate sainthood, the ideal of Christianity, is Unconditional Love: 540. Where can you find 540 in today's society? There are spiritual teachers above 540. There are spiritual groups 540 and over—the best known being Alcoholics Anonymous. AA, curiously enough, calibrates at 540,

Unconditional Love. Unconditional Love, which is shocking to people who are not familiar with Unconditional Love—because a guy has a slip; he goes out and shoots three people, runs over five children, and burns down his house. And when he comes back to a meeting, they say, "Gee, we're glad you're back, Joe. You sure need to be here. You may not think you've got a problem, but we know you do." That is Unconditional Love in practice as a reality— not as a religious ideal to be memorized, but as an actual way of the heart.

Jesus says that if you get up to 540, you really don't have to worry; in fact, He says if you get up to 500, you don't have to worry—the ideal of "Love your neighbor as yourself." "It's over 500: resist" (True). "It's over 540: resist" (True). It's Unconditional Love. I hate to tell you, but it's Unconditional Love.

Where does the willingness come from? As justified as it is, you realize what it's costing you. You say, "Do I love Jesus, do I love Christ, do I love God? Am I willing to sacrifice the ego for Enlightenment more than I want to dislike this person?" And of course, the answer becomes, "No." Otherwise, you're giving your ultimate spiritual destiny to some stranger—your ex-mother-in-law, or something. You understand? So, the willingness to surrender, then, comes out of the willingness to give all to God.

Ramana Maharshi is well-known because he only died in 1958. The advantage of the more recent gurus who calibrate in the 700s—Nisargadatta Maharaj and Ramana Maharshi are both around 700—is because they lived so relatively recently that we at least have verbatim some explanations of teachings which were already there in more cryptic form hundreds of years or even a thousand years ago, but they were so cryptic as to be unintelligible unless you are already enlightened. Many of the things that are said, let's say, by Huang Po are absolutely right on. But to realize they're right on, you've got to be at, like, 800 to get it, which isn't too helpful when you're still trying to figure out how to forgive your ex-mother-in-law.

Practically speaking, we want to start with a teacher to whom we can relate. Having a teacher with a very high calibration is not necessarily of any great benefit. I think the aura of the great teacher is a great benefit, but the specifics of what is being taught may not correlate with where you are at the time. If you are still having trouble forgiving your ex-mother-in-law, you don't need a teacher at 800 to tell you that you've got to let that go. *A Course in Miracles* is extremely good at that, because *A Course in Miracles* says you cannot forgive it as you presently see it. Isn't that a great, brilliant observation on the nature of the ego? The way you see it now, no, you can't honestly, legitimately let it go. You can only pretend to let it go. You can only suppress the anger. You can only suppress the judgmentalism. It says that your problem is not that you hated her or you are angry, or something. The problem is that reality has been distorted by the perceptual apparatus of the ego, and now you're seeing it out of context. When you place it back in context, it's automatically resolved—there's nothing to forgive. Every negative feeling, then, is a consequence of taking something out of context—taking it out of context and coloring it with an emotionality.

So, how do you surrender the ego? First, contextualize what ego really is, that it's not evil and that it's the persistence of the animal; but persistence of the animal deters one's spiritual evolution and therefore, the object is to transcend it. The best way to transcend it, and the reason for these lectures, is to describe in some detail the actual mechanisms of the ego. In *A Course in Miracles*, that is done to a considerable extent. There is a considerable explanation, as you go through the workbook, of the mechanisms of the ego. But then it's really up to the Holy Spirit. When you surrender it to God, you are asking God to recontextualize it so that you see it differently. Now that you see it differently, there's nothing to forgive and the whole thing is resolved. In these lectures we try to be more specific about how that perceptual distortion occurs in the first place. It occurs in the first place because of the ego's propensity for positionality—positionality meaning the creation of the opposites by an arbitrary point of view. To pick on a scale of temperature and say, "Above this is hot and below this is cold." Well, you could have gone down here and said, "Above this is hot and below this is cold." Or you could have gone up here and say, "Above this is hot, and below here is cold." The important thing to see is that the scale is really only of *one* measurement. It's not two. It's not either/or. It's not good versus bad. To see that what the mind considers to be opposites are merely gradations all on the same scale.

Let's take what could be conceived of by the ego as a duality in this very scale of consciousness. We could say there's a duality between that which is above 200 and makes you go strong with kinesiology, and that which is below 200 and makes you go weak. Like temperature—temperature measures the presence of heat. It doesn't measure the presence of cold. There's only one variable, called "heat." If heat is present, we call it "warm." As less and less heat is present, we call it "cold." So, cold is nothing but the absence of heat, right? There is no such thing as coldness.

We can do the same thing with light. Light and darkness are not opposites. There is only one variable. Light is either present or not. Light is either intensely present—less and less light, we begin to say it's getting dimmer; now we can say it's semidark; now we can say it's dark; now we can say it's pitch-black. There's not two variables called "light" and "darkness." Therein lies the resolution of the problems of the ego. To realize that one thing: there is only *one* variable. It's present to varying degrees, that's all; or experienceable by varying degrees.

So, on this scale of consciousness, then, the light which shines forth is first described in Genesis—the Unmanifest becomes manifest in the nonlinear world of non-form as the energy field of light, representing the infinite potentiality of that which becomes the universe. As the infinite potentiality, the Radiance of God shines forth as creation. It does so first in the nonlinear domain. Only way down the whole process does it begin to appear in form and materiality. That's way along the process by the time it reaches physicality. Then the light interacts with physicality, and life originates and then evolves from the bottom up.

There's no conflict between evolution and creation, because evolution *is* creation. So as the hand of God unfolds, perception witnesses it as a sequence in what it thinks is "time." But all we're seeing is the unfoldment of creation, and therefore creation is what is responsible for what is happening this instant, because the unfoldingness of creation is what we call "now."

All we see, then, is the infinite potentiality of the power of God, manifesting not only as this universe but as an infinite sequence of universes, because the essence of God includes, as a quality, creation, creativity. That which is created by God then has the essence of God within it and consequently also has the power of creation. So, as we speak of it linguistically, out of the universe arises an infinite universe of infinite universes of infinite universes which, every instant, faster than the speed of light, are creating further universes, which—because they are innately creative—are creating other universes. You understand what I am saying?

Out of power like that, we have to scale down the power so that it's compatible with protoplasmic life. This kind of energy, then, would fry an ordinary piece of protoplasm, wouldn't it? It even boils solid rock into lava. So, Infinite Power gets scaled down. This is a scale of Love. At the top is Infinite, Unconditional Love, and this lower level represents less and less Love. When we get down to the level of the dinosaur, Love is sorely absent. The dinosaur does not really care about another as he gobbles him up. You see, maybe the most advanced dinosaur, she lays an egg and maybe passes back a longing glance at it at the beginning. But she goes on, because there are other things to do.

So, we see consciousness then can be calibrated as to the presence of Love. This lower section denotes the absence of Love. As we note the absence of Love, we notice that instead of Love, we have egocentricity. We have a narcissistic, megalomanic self-aggrandizement in which the self (with a small *s*) of the ego becomes God; and out of that, to maintain that illusion, that which is really God has to be refused. And that's why the lower astral realm arises. The lower astral realm is constituted by that consciousness which refuses the Divinity of God as Creator and says no. "I'm Milošević and greater than all of mankind, and the International Tribunal has no right to question my actions; nor do these judges have any authority, nor does this court have any existing authority, because I am greater than all of mankind." Right? "I can therefore with impunity slaughter 34 million people. And it's my business, not yours." It allows Hitler to say that the Germans don't deserve to live, because they lost the war; and he wanted all of Germany destroyed, right? He wanted all of Paris destroyed.

Throughout history, that which is totally devoid of Divine Love, and refuses it, presents itself on the planet as evil. "What I'm thinking is correct: resist" (True). "It's okay to say it right here" (True). The dinosaurs, as much as they're cute and we give them away with hamburgers and all, are the ultimate—the killers of mankind, the opposite way of the herbivore. Love appears within evolution first as maternal love; that's its first breakthrough. So, the evolution into Love—choosing would be the Love, choosing God; or choosing the negative god and choosing the energy of the dinosaur—is like two alternate ways to go.

The degree to which Love is present, then, and the unconditionality of it, the willingness to totally surrender anything and everything to God, is the one variable on that scale. It does not mean that anybody is better than anybody else. That's why I like the other scale. It's mathematically correct, but it doesn't infer what we're saying.

The Presence of God is infinite potentiality. It's a reality of the Self unfolding. This is the persistence, you might say, of the animal world, the persistence of the animal domain. There's two ways to go: the way of hatred and the dinosaur, where your survival is always at the cost of the life of someone else, or the way of the herbivore in which life is sustained in the mammalian world by Love. So, you choose either Love or non-Love.

The freedom of our own nature as we are created is to choose God or not. I spent many years as an atheist. I was a devout atheist. I didn't fool around with it as an intellectual position because it was cute and stylish. As I've spoken before, I was walking in the woods one day, and I was a devout—in fact, a scrupulous—Christian. I was a boy soprano, and I still adore church and great cathedrals. I don't speak in great cathedrals, because the minute I walk in, I break out in tears at the incredible beauty of it. Anyway, one day I was walking through the woods, and all of a sudden, the totality of man's suffering was revealed. It was almost like the opposite side of the infinite light that came to me when I was, like, 37 or whatever. It was almost like the opposite of it—the totality of the suffering of all mankind throughout all of time. I can't explain to you how I knew it, but it was. In that instant I became an atheist. I hated any god that could allow the sheer dimension, as well as qualities, of what I saw. I became a *rabid* atheist. I went to Jesuit universities, and when you hit the bar on Friday night—I mean I could beat 'em, beat their socks off with theology. I got a straight A in theology, and thought it was all BS. Hahaha, so here's this atheist getting straight As in theology. I could tell you everything that's wrong with Thomas Aquinas's proof for the existence of God as primary cause. In fact, I can tell you today, if I remember. And I would always go there for the free beer. Those drinking days are gone.

Because I held a confusion which the ego commonly makes. It holds God responsible for that which is the consequence of the ego. The totality of human suffering is a consequence of all those ego positions. It's not a consequence of God. God doesn't create anything like that, but the ego does create it. So I held God responsible for that which is really the consequence of the functioning of the ego.

But I was integrously atheist. Let's see what happens to the atheist, calibration-wise. "At the level of the atheist, the integrity was over 200" (True); "210" (True); "280"

(True); "300" (Not true). All right. So, the atheist can be integrous. Integrous, if it is not an intellectual position of pridefulness and vanity and ego. But if one's commitment to truth is profound and you are a religionist, there's going to be a moment when you're going to go through a violent convulsion, because a lot of what one holds dear is going to run smack up against commitment to absolute truth. And that's what happened with me.

At the time I was in psychoanalysis and Lionel Ovesey was a professor at Columbia University, and he was an atheist too, so we took a dim view of religion. He called it "foxhole fear," and I said, "You're right! Regress to childhood, and you want Daddy God to save you." We both ridiculed it. So that's as good as the intellect can do with God, because the Presence of God is a direct and profound experience. And all that went out the window many years later when I hit bottom and the ego stopped functioning altogether—went into a funk.

So the willingness to surrender every positionality to God requires understanding the nature of the ego. We've said the ego works on the basis of positionalities of either/ or. It takes that which is unitary and tries to dissolve it into a duality. So, the problem of the ego is that positionality creates duality. Therefore, the strict definition of the pathway which I represent would be most closely, historically, Advaita, the pathway of understanding the Presence of God by understanding the nature and the source of the mind itself. Which takes you, as you go through it, beyond mind to "no-mind," and then the question is, "How do you explain 'no-mind' in language?" That took 30 years: how to explain "no-mind" via the "mind."

The willingness to surrender positionalities—the power behind it is really the heart. The willingness to surrender the way you see it and ask God to show it to you as it is in truth, the willingness to let go right and wrong—this part is important. The rest of it is just talking. What keeps these positions in place is the satisfaction and the feedback we get out of it—the juice we get out of it. The ego can juice any situation and just suck all kinds of continuing energy to survive out of it—the evening news at 5:30, as we talked about earlier.

The Test of the Tempter

The difference between hot and cold, as you can see, is an artificial positionality. So your intellect sees it. But, no, the problem is going to be emotional—that you get grim satisfaction out of everything: grim satisfaction out of martyrdom, out of being wronged. The more horribly you're wronged, let me tell you, the bigger the juice. The more horrible the crime committed against you, the more stuck you are in your ego now, because the payoff is big. The payoff gets bigger and bigger. And as you evolve spiritually, the tempter is going to come to you, and the way the tempter comes to you is offering an enormous gratification of a justified position. At a certain consciousness level, the tempter comes to you.

You might say, that which we call "the tempter" is present at all times; you're constantly under the test of "the tempter," if you want to call it that. What's the source of the tempter? The source of the tempter, then, is the pleasure one derives out of one's ego positionalities. It isn't power over others; it's the gratification you get out of power over others. What the hell do these idiots who slaughter millions get out of it? They don't even get to see it, right? Hey, there are millions of people getting slaughtered and chopped up out there, and you don't even get to see it; you're locked up in your office here. Look what you're missing. Get out there and slosh around in the blood and step over the bodies! I mean, you're missing the grim, satanic satisfaction. No, the satisfaction he's getting out of it is Luciferic, not satanic. Satanic is the expression, but what he's coming out of is power over others, the capacity to be God over others. That's Milošević—look at him on TV. The pridefulness of that positionality is what he's unwilling to relinquish to God. And that's how you choose the lower astral: positionality.

So, you'll catch the ego red-handed. You'll see that he gets a grim satisfaction to say, "Oh, I can't possibly be enjoying this suffering." No, you're not enjoying the suffering; you're enjoying the juice you're getting out of the suffering. Do you get what I am saying about "juice"? The ego feeds off the juice it gets out of what otherwise—at least to the intellect—is described as negative. No sooner is the town demolished by the flowing lava than they're rebuilding a new one exactly in the same place. Isn't that right? No sooner does the house slide down the side of the mountain into the Pacific Ocean than they're building a new one, in exactly the same place. No sooner do the rivers flow over the banks in the Midwest and sweep millions of houses away, they're instantly building houses as soon as the mud dries.

The ego's attraction and addiction is to the juice it gets out of suffering and being mistreated. That's the juice of the far-left, liberal, politically correct position: that you can get juice out of any social reality by recontextualizing it. Why? Because the egotism involved brings you to a position called "entitlement." Once you're entitled, everything is an offense. Everything is an offense. Everything

is a possible lawsuit. Everything is publicity, because entitlement is the grandiosity of the ego, of the infant. So,
egomania is nothing but the grandiosity of the unbridled
infant of the ego. Expecting the world to acknowledge it,
the king baby inside. It expects the world to cater to its
egocentric position. The world never heard of you, and
after you've left, it's not going to miss you. The idea that
it's going to cater to you while you're here is about a three-
month-old's positionality. But the juice that's derived out
of the indignities and injustices of this world—it *thrives* on
it. All the people that are rude to you.

No sooner did they catch this crazy butcher of 30 people who chops them up, and I won't even tell you—it's
unspeakable what he did to the remnants of their bodies. No sooner does this happen than some poppycock
jumps up on TV—he's worried about the civil rights of this
sucker. Right. Why? Because he can milk injustice out of
this. He can see the position of the winner is always "the
bad guy." Like the capitalist is always "the bad guy." Who
says that? A guy wearing clothes? Yes. Where did you get
your clothes? "Well, [they were] manufactured by some
company." Where did the company get its money? It got it
from capital, didn't it? You're walking on a sidewalk. Who
made that sidewalk? Some company made the sidewalk.
You sit in a car. Who made your car? You open your bottle
of milk in the morning. Where did you get the milk? You
got it from some company. Where did you get the money
to buy all these things that the people you hate provided
for you? Well, you got it from the people you hate, because
they provided the jobs, right?

So, you see how positionality makes everything wrong.
You can make the goose who lays the golden egg the bad
guy. So positionalities swing back and forth, then, and

create the political spectrum which keeps us entertained. All the guys in the restaurant in the morning look forward to opening the editorial page. What's today's outrageous calamity that you can really discuss with the other guys, and how stupid the government is, and all. So when you are honest about it, you see that you love your ego. You love the juice you get out of your ego. See? Once you admit that truth, you've taken the cover off of it. You *love* the ego. It's your source of juice; it's the source of all the injustices, the calamities, the pains, the hatreds. Where would you be without it? You'd be stuck with the reality of the Self, which doesn't buy that crap. It doesn't buy it at all. Give me a break! That's what God says when people say, "What have you got to say, God?" God says: "Give me a break! Give me a break. Enough from all this human juice! Take away the TV set. I looked at it and you can have it back." I gave God a TV set, and He said, "I don't want to look at it—it's horrible." Why? Because it's full of all this juice that we get out of it.

The movies juice you to death, you know. If you calibrate a lot of commercials, TV commercials and a lot of movies, your arm will go weak about 14 times a minute. Why? Because we love the fear, we love the indignation, we love the shock, gore, horror.

It Takes Radical Honesty to Undo the Ego

The way to undo the ego is radical honesty. The way of Advaita is radical truth: the willingness to let go all illusions, including the illusions about illusions. The source of the ego, then, is the juice that we continuously get out of it, which pumps it up; pumps it up, pumps it up; gives it life. The willingness to relinquish that, that's what you have to surrender to God. Not positionality, because the minute you let go the secondary gain that you're getting out of that position, the ego positionality will disappear of itself. You'll laugh at it. It will let go of itself. The thing to search for is: "What kind of satisfaction do I get out of that?" I get the satisfaction of being wronged. "Wronged" is wonderful, is it not? Whole countries go to war, and they're wronged. They're righting the wrong of Versailles. What wrong of Versailles? The kaiser did the same thing that Hitler did and lost. Now Hitler says that was an injustice. What injustice? Nobody asked the kaiser to invade Europe and kill people, did they?

So, it feeds off that injustice. The whole German people—40 million people died in World War II. I was in World War II, and it's more of a reality to me than [to] many younger people. It was a reality in which 70 million people died, out of the juice, out of the juice of being wronged.

The pleasure that one gets out of the juice of the ego justifies everything. It justifies mass murder; genocide; if allowed to, the final killer bomb if they lost the war. The final killer bomb was big enough to eliminate all of mankind. All of mankind was going to be eliminated by the final killer bomb if Russia lost a nuclear war with the United States. Luckily, there were enough Russians to stop them before it became a reality, but the megalomania behind it, as you see, is unstoppable.

The difficulty with the reasonable ego of the Western world is that it presumes that other people are going to operate within the lawful confines and reasonableness of the ego. Other people are not. People say, "Well, he wouldn't do that. It would cost him all his countrymen." Of course he would do that!

So, the weakness of our position as you see it in the world is the presumption by the naive that other people are going to be ruled by reason. The 400s is the level of reason. We say, "Well, nobody would do that; that's irrational." There are lots of people in the world that think rationality is stupid. You want something, you take it, man—what's the problem? There are whole cultures. You know how that culture thinks: "Well, she left her purse there, so she deserves it." I treat them all week long—Monday, Wednesday, and Friday morning. "If I can get away with it, they deserved it" is the justification. In the 400s, you don't buy that, but down in the lower part of the world, that's justified.

"They deserve to die because they are killable." Whoa! Do you realize what that means when people come from that space? Because they're killable—that's why they deserve to die. The dinosaur doesn't need justification to eat the smaller animal. He kills it because it's chewable, I guess. So now you understand a little bit more about the ego.

You don't have to be afraid of it. You have to be honest that it's there. And that it owes its survival to the payoff it gets out of its positions. The payoff—the way to get rid of it is, first, be honest and admit it. "Yeah, I enjoy . . . whatever. Now, am I willing to let that enjoyment go for some higher purpose?" Well, you can only take the word of people who have done so whether the sacrifice is worth it. Because it does seem to the ego to sacrifice all of that glory and fame and justification and revenge and all is a big sacrifice. Don't kid yourself. To the ego, it is a big sacrifice. It is a big sacrifice to let go "being right," to let go . . . not nurturing that wrong, to let go of that hatred. It is a big sacrifice—don't pretend it's a small sacrifice. There's a lot of pseudo, nongenuine spiritual work that people attempt, and it doesn't work. Why? Because they are unwilling to face the nitty-gritty, the nitty-gritty facts.

Radical truth means you've got to take the mask off everything and be willing to see it for what it is, and now handle it from the viewpoint of emotional honesty. There is a big, massive payoff in ego positions, or you wouldn't be sitting here in a body today. You would have karmically gone off into the mists of the higher realms. And therefore, the fact that one is back here in a body again means that one *has* sold out spiritual truth for the gratifications of the ego over and over again. But in this lifetime, it's coming up to be questioned. In this lifetime, you say, "Was it worth it? Is the experience of the Presence of God worth sacrificing all that I get out of my ego?" The answer can only be gotten by faith, actually. Experientially, no. Experientially, you've got nothing upon which to say that giving it up would be a better deal. Anything in your experience telling you that giving up the pleasure, resentments, and hatreds and satisfactions of winning is worth it? Not experientially, no. Faith, yes. Based on faith. Based on the teaching of some entity who has gone through the whole trip and tells you that the end result, the experience of God, is so incredible, beyond all description—so beyond the totality of all the values of all of mankind throughout all of history. All the pleasures and all the values and all the acquisitions, emotionally and materially of all of mankind throughout all of history, are like a speck compared to the Presence of God. Nothing is even in the same domain. Therefore, you're asked to sacrifice that with which you are familiar in hopes of entering a different domain. And in that domain, you only have the traveler that's been there. Marco Polo tells you what the Chinese are like, but you have to take his word for it.

So, we have the inspiration, then, of the spiritual teacher. The value of the guru is primarily one of commitment to absolute truth, out of which comes an integrity which is so profound and convincing that one buys that integrity. See, truth cannot be argued. It cannot be defended, and it has no answers for any argument. Its authority is absolute. It is the Absoluteness of the Presence that defies any question and against which any question falls flat, because there is no room for question. That which is All That Is is beyond all questioning.

To let go and surrender the known for the unknown— we call it the Institute for Advanced Spiritual Research. Every spiritual aspirant is a researcher. You have no idea what you're really going to experience when you let a certain thing go. You only find it by doing it. You only find it by doing it. Just like the explorer, you can go by the compass, but you don't really know until you get there that that's an absolute fact. So, each one of us evolves based on faith. The faith of the conviction of the integrity of whatever spiritual teacher or church or spiritual tradition, whatever guru, whatever. One's inner direction leads one to that which you're able to hang on to with absolute certainty. When I was an atheist, I'd already got the absolute certainty of the truth of the Buddha. I was an atheist at the time, and I knew that what he said was absolutely so. So the intuitive knowingness was there, many years prior to the validation experientially.

Karma Is What You Are

That leads us up to the next topic, which is the part karma plays in all of this. To avoid the whole subject of karma is, again, the fallacy of many religious positions which say, "I don't believe in karma." I don't want anybody to believe in karma at all. I don't want *anybody* to believe in karma.

I don't believe in karma. Karma is what you *are*. You ask, "How do you let go of the ego?" Well, the ego *is* the accumulated karma of all of life through all of time, through all of history as it presents itself now in the reality of that which you are at this moment. Somebody says they don't believe in karma; in that case, you don't exist, because you've got two ears, two eyes, a nose, and a mouth. If that ain't karmic, what is it? I mean, you didn't come up with four ears and three eyes and two mouths, you know. So obviously, this moment then represents the accumulated energies and effects in form throughout all of time.

You can't pretend that somehow the evolution of consciousness throughout all of time and throughout all forms of life has somehow bypassed you and you have magically escaped karma. No way. That's spiritual pride to think that one is not subject to the laws of the universe.

One time in a very advanced state—it was a very, very advanced state—came the potential downfall of the guru. A lot of gurus fall down. "At the pass was over 800" (True); "820" (True); "840" (True); "860" (Not true). Around 850. So, it's another shocking fact. You see, to be a radical realist takes a lot of guts. It takes a lot of guts and takes a lot of heart. You've got to face radical facts about things you don't want to face. Many well-known gurus, if you calibrate their writings, they're pretty good. If you calibrate where they were at, at the height of their spiritual evolution, you get a very good number. If you ask where they are at now, you may get a very low number. Shock. Because at each point along the way, it's like a test comes up that says, "Oh, yeah?" The students I teach are unprepared for that. First of all, don't pretend it's not going to happen, because it's going to happen. You say, "I'm never going to 'so-and-so' again." The next question that comes up from the universe is, "Oh, yeah? Oh, yeah?" "Uh huh." "Yeah, sure." Anyway, this was a very advanced state, and it was a state of absolute purity and a profound state of the Presence as clarity, peace, and non-positionality. Anyway, in this state, which was nonverbal, because thought had stopped years before that, came a knowingness that presented itself. The knowingness was, "Now that you have transcended karma and are no longer answerable to some otherness called 'God,' and you realize there is no otherness to which you are answerable for; and because you realize you are beyond all human karma, you are not answerable in human terms, all power resides in you. Own it." That was the temptation, the ultimate Luciferic power for its own sake. And the rationale was correct up to a certain level. When you truly transcend the ego, you're not subject to human karma and normal human karmic terms; nor is there some angry god that you are going to face who is going to get even with you for being bad and beat you up and throw you into hell. All that's bullshit. Anyway, you've transcended all that.

Now, knowing all that, how about this: you *are* the power. Here comes the Luciferic temptation. And you could see who had said yes and who had said no. It was strange. Not all that many had been through, and you could see who said yes and who said no. Power for its own sake. You say to yourself, "Why would that which we call 'evil,' by the world's terms, choose to be that way?" It does it for the payoff—for the sake of power itself. Not because the power gets you something, but for its own sake. Just as people will murder, not for some motive; looking for psychological reasons why the thrill killer kills is totally absurd. "He got beat up in his childhood." Yeah, right! Everybody got beat up in his childhood. No, he does it for the sake of *it* itself. He murders for the sake of the thrill of murdering.

The way we surrender the ego, then, is we're radically honest, we're radically honest. We see the payoff we get out of it. We are radically honest about whether we are actually willing to give up that payoff for something promised but not yet experienced, because that takes faith.

What is karma, really? How far does it go? See, the error that was made by that Luciferic energy at that level was, it's beyond the karma of the ego but not beyond the karma of the Reality of the universe. You are not beyond the reality of the karma of God, of the Reality of the universe, which is far beyond the human. It includes you in it! So, if I'd known what to say to that entity at the time, I would have turned on him and said, "And that includes you." Unless you're greater than the Infinite Reality of the Infinite Creator of universes of universes, out of which your little silliness arose. Anyway, those are some things that happen to you and is pertinent to karma, and we will talk more about karma later.

The Process of Letting Go Takes Intention

How do you not revert? Well, many things are let go of in degrees, you see. And you've accumulated pressure of many lifetimes behind many things. So, it's more than just a passing thought, sometimes. It takes very intense intention and devotion and the miraculous to let it go. And that's why prayer and the request for intercession is traditional: to ask God for help to let go my addictions and the pleasure I am getting out of such and such a thing, see. So we ask for Divine help. That is the pathway of devotion.

To understand spiritual work, it's necessary to know something about karma and what is the truth of karma. What does it really mean? First of all, it's somewhat stigmatized among Christian circles and others as being of Eastern origin and therefore foreign, and all this and that. Karma as a specific religious concept, of course, is defined in the dictionary in a very specific way. Karma, in my understanding, is more the essence of karma in that All That Is, the entire universe, in fact all the universes of universes—is one karmic totality. One karmic symphony. In other words, all that ever existed, all that ever is—in thought, word, or deed in both the linear and nonlinear domains—are part of a total oneness. To be beyond karma would mean that somehow you escaped the oneness of the totality of God and all the universes, which is not likely.

The universe is one karmic unity in perfect and total balance, in every detail. All That Is is obviously part of the evolution of all that was at the point of observation, becoming the fulfillment of its innate propensity which was created as part of creation. Everything is perfect because at every point, it is fulfilling its potentiality as it is possible for that potentiality to unfold under the conditions that we call "the present." In the next instant, it will again be perfect. So, all is perfect at every instant. The only way to make it not perfect is to contextualize it in the hypothetical. But because the hypothetical has no reality, it does not invalidate the truth of what was just said. The hypothetical does not exist.

So, because the universe is one karmic unity in a continuous state of perfection of the unfolding of its potentiality, nothing can escape karma and still be part of the universe. So, if anything was beyond karma, you wouldn't know about it. There is no point to worry about it, because it wouldn't exist, and neither would you. You cannot be anything this instant unless you were something the last instant.

How does it operate, really, spiritually speaking? First of all, the confusion has to do with confusing karma with reincarnation. The reason it's rejected by Christian belief systems is because of two things: that Jesus Christ did not talk about it, and specifically, it's referring to embodiment. Generally, karma as understood by the common layman is: if you're not good, you will come back as a toad; or you are a very good toad, and now you are not a toad anymore. So it's confused with incarnation. Now, karma and incarnation are two different things. Reincarnation can be a karmic potentiality, or it may not. Karma is merely stating that that which is continuous is continuous, and part of an ongoing Oneness. What it is really saying spiritually is that the decisions of the spiritual will then have consequences. These consequences are agreed upon by all religions. Those who claim they don't believe in karma—of course they believe in karma. Otherwise, why would you avoid sin? Because after you die, karmically you are going to go to other places. So they all believe in karma, but they don't believe in reincarnation. That's two different things.

Karma means that the consequences of actions will have an effect in the future. And of course, Christ taught that. "You reap as you sow," et cetera. So, He taught karma, but He did not get into the whole problem of embodiment. Karmically, embodiment is a very complicated and tricky question. It may or may not occur, and it may or may not be an option, and it may or may not be said yes to.

The other thing that people don't understand about karma is that there's an infinite number of universes. There is an infinite number of domains. Within an infinite number of domains, there's an infinite potentiality of infinite universes, and these multiply at an infinite rate. I want you to wrap yourself around *that* one! I want to ask a question that's been bugging me. "I may ask this question: resist" (True). "Jesus Christ never had any previous physical incarnations. I may ask that: resist" (True). "That is a fact: resist" (True). "The Buddha did: resist" (True). That's what I thought. I was driving along the other day and I thought, *One reason Jesus Christ didn't talk about previous embodiments is because He never had any.* The Buddha, however, did. And by level 600, you recall 'em; not that they are different lifetimes, but it's just like a memory—like you remember what your teacher said in eighth grade.

So, Jesus Christ, first of all, came directly from heaven, see. He never incarnated as a human physicality. "Jesus never incarnated as a physicality before: resist" (True). That's one thing I like about kinesiology. You ask these questions, and after you've asked thousands of them, it weaves a fabric of understanding that is greater in depth and dimension and subtlety than can be easily described. I always thought, until this moment, that Jesus Christ didn't go into the subject of karma specifically—past-life karma—because the ego as it is today *is* the karma. Your karma is today's ego. Today's ego is the compilation of all that has occurred in the evolution of this consciousness up to this moment, just like a tomato is. A tomato sitting here represents the evolution of tomato-ness throughout all of time until it is manifesting as this tomato. There is no way this tomato can escape tomato karma, because it *is* tomato karma.

The ego of today is nothing but the crystallization and manifestation in this lifetime of all that has been accumulated since the beginning of time by this particular consciousness. Because they're one and the same, I thought Jesus Christ's understanding and seeing that equality, there's no point in talking about past lives and confusing people. Because at the time that He incarnated and the culture in which He incarnated, it would have been another excuse to reject His teaching as outlandish, because in traditional Judaism, past lives is not taught. So He would have been more out of gear with the society in which He got Himself born.

The Buddha, on the other hand, not only recalled them but also taught in a society in which that was common knowledge. That's common knowledge in the Far East—that one has had numerous incarnations and, hopefully, up the evolutionary tree.

Then we'd say that every act of the will, every assent of the Spiritual Will, is reflected in one's spiritual—the vibrational energy field called the "Soul." Let's see if what we just said is so. We'll check everything out: "That's so: resist" (True). Thank you. See, I don't care whether it's so or not. Usually you get a question: how do you know that what you're doing is scientifically accurate? I don't frankly care. I really don't care; nor do I care if people are unable to do it or just believe in it. It's just a tool, you understand what I'm saying, but it's an extremely informational tool, extremely informational, pretty much like a compass, you know. To navigate without a compass is where mankind has been. Mankind has been unable to know truth from falsehood.

The inability to know truth from falsehood is why the millions get slaughtered, generation after generation. One incredible monster after another slaughters more millions. And they never lack for followers. Somehow, they never lack for followers. No matter how bizarre it is, you'll find endless followers, you know.

The Spiritual Will Determines One's Karma

"One's karmic position is determined by the agreement of the Spiritual Will: resist" (True). All right. So, it's the Spiritual Will, then, which determines one's karma. That which you spiritually intend to be, the result is what determines one's karmic fate.

How does the karma operate, then, and how can you say that the justice of God is absolute? It's obvious when you go into a certain state. It is a condition. Enlightenment is a condition. What kind of condition would you call it? It's a paradigm. The ego has one paradigm, and that's the paradigm of the linear. The nonlinear is just a different paradigm. From this paradigm, this paradigm seems unreal or outlandish, and to the scientific world, not believable. To this paradigm, this viewpoint is equally untenable. Anyway, because the universe is a karmic unity, you could say that which is the infinite power of the Unmanifest becomes manifest as the universe; creates a karmic field, let's say, within the Absolute Reality and the infinite power of God would be like an enormous electromagnetic field, and everything is included within it.

When we explain the difference between power and force—force is something that goes from "here" to "there" and expends energy and therefore comes to an end. Power does not require any input of energy, is beyond time, and stands there and holds all within its field without the requirement of any energy. And because it is just the field, everything in it aligns itself within that field according to that which it is. So if you're a little iron filing, then, where you're standing in this electromagnetic field depends on the strength of your charge, your shape, the negative and positive poles and where they are, et cetera. So, what you've become by virtue of spiritual agreement, by virtue of the Spiritual Will, then, has determined the charge on your spiritual body, which, as it separates from the physical body, will automatically gravitate where it's destined to be by virtue of that which it has become. By virtue of that which it has become, it will automatically adjust itself to where it belongs within the infinite magnetic field of the Will of God. Yeah? Is that simple enough? It does not require any arbitrary God or Judgment Day, because the consequence of that which you are is automatic as the consequence of the reality of that which it is. There's no arbitrary God who has to sit up there and wait until you get up there and, boy, you're going to get it. It's absolutely not necessary.

That which chooses and is attracted by hatred goes to the realms of hatred. That which is attracted by beauty and peace and Love and Divinity automatically gravitates to it. Is that in agreement and obvious? Therefore, the judgment of God is absolute, and absolutely perfect, by the virtue of the nature of Creation itself. All of Creation, then, in its perfection guarantees absolute justice. Nothing and no one will go to any place other than that which it already is. That's pretty clear, yes? Like a cork in water, then, each one floats depending on one's buoyancy and the density of the water. Salt water is denser.

Therefore, one can refuse the sovereignty of God, and refuse God, and choose the lower astral realms. God doesn't force you to accept God; nor does God force you to the lower astral realms. People gravitate toward hatred because that is what they have chosen.

Everyone Starts from Where They Are—There Is No Punitive Judge

We would assume that a run-down, degenerate-looking bar and grill, with drunks lying around the place and vermin in the place and rats eating the garbage, that the people who go there would love it when they clean it up and paint it and put new drapes and get rid of the rats and disarm the patrons. And we all know that's not a fact. The new owner comes in, cleans up the place with new drapes, new carpets. The old crowd doesn't go there at all. They desert it. Remember the Electric Circus in the East Village—that was early '60s; it was the beginning of the psychedelic era. It was the "in" place to go. Andy Warhol and all the elite intellectual, artistic types went to the Electric Circus—and the groups that later became famous, they weren't famous then. That was the first psychedelic disco. The walls had just drapes, because they didn't have money for walls and stuff. It was hip, cool, and everybody who was anybody went there. After a year or two, I forget, some new owner bought it. They closed it for about two months while they cleaned it up. Well, they cleaned it up, and now it had curvilinear, beautiful plastic walls and stuff, and nobody went there. The fact that it was funky was why it was cool and a lot of people liked it. You know what I'm sayin'? They cleaned up the old Electric Circus, and it fell on its butt. Nobody went there anymore. It was no longer hip, wasn't cool, nobody wanted it.

So, as amazing as it would be to people in the 400s, there are people who *prefer* to be on the streets. I'm in charge of a treatment center, and a lot of them, the minute you let them out, they'll go right back to the very source of their own devastation. Right back—exactly the same lifestyle, same people. Just as the wife goes back to the man who beats her up—she gets a court-order protection, and within 48 hours, she's back with him and then he's beating her up again. So it goes, over and over; the person is attracted to that which they are karmically destined for.

So that pretty much takes care of some of the questions we had there, because it takes the view of God as judge. You might say, the universe judges absolutely, but not in the moral, arbitrary, ego understanding of the word *judge*. The idea of the judge, the punitive judge, comes from, really, the Old Testament. The Old Testament itself arises from tribal gods. See, all the early cultures had tribal gods. There are the Roman gods and the Greek gods, and they all have great names—Zeus and Athena and all these various gods—and they were supplanted over time as life evolved. Some of the early scriptures still have these anthropomorphic gods who are subject to all the fallacies and foibles of the human ego. The so-called gods of many ancient cultures are nothing but exaggerated humans subject to the same proclivities of the ego—jealousy and envy and hatred and revenge and vanity. But when you calibrate their energy, you see they're mostly the so-called gods of the lower astral realms. They're talking about the gods of the lower astral realms, who rule by vanity and egotism and revenge and anger and favoritism. So you're not talking about the God of the evolution of consciousness; you're talking about gods of the lower astral realms, right? Freud said they're all projections from the unconscious. Let's see what we say about it. "The gods that I was talking about are projections from the unconscious: resist" (True). Okay. "They also exist as 'realities,' in quotes, in lower astral realms: resist" (True). "Because they got projected there: resist" (True). So, they originated in the unconscious out of guilt, fear, anger, hatred, and all those things. And they're accepted as realities by a large part of society. A large part of society doesn't know which end of this chart God is at. You talk about spiritual confusion. Large parts of society—and I say large parts, very large parts of society—think God is down here. I don't know what they think is up there. There's one religious group that thinks that to experience the Buddha nature is a demon and that God is down here. Even if you can't tell the top of the chart from the bottom of the chart, you really ought to not proselytize others, you know. I mean, you can do damage to your own karmic potentiality, but to drag others along with you . . . proselytizing has never been something I have been interested in.

Karmic propensity, then, means that as a result of whatever has gone on, you start from where you are at. Everybody has to start from where they're at. Where you are is from where you were. In a Christian culture, for those who believe in karma, they have usually been influenced by Buddhic things and by their own personal experiences to a qualified karmic understanding of karma that, no doubt, what you do in this lifetime is going to have quite profound consequences in the future, which may or may not include the choice to reincarnate. The implied purpose of reincarnation is the chance to choose again, the chance to choose again. And many spiritual teachings do emphasize that this is a chance to choose again. Doesn't *A Course in Miracles* call it that? "What *A Course in Miracles* says about this is a fact: resist" (True). "People who incarnate now have chosen to incarnate: resist" (True). "They were forced to incarnate: resist" (Not true). None of us were forced to. I didn't know that. "We were given an option to choose again: resist" (True). "Many of us choose to undo by re-experiencing what we did to others: resist" (True). Yes. I know my own consciousness before this event that happened was one that would choose to experience that which I did to someone else, because I didn't see any other way to undo it. So, the guilt of that which I did was sufficient that I was actually willing to re-experience exactly what I did to that other person, you see. I gave the example of not killing somebody that I should have killed, haha, and going through a hernia repair without anesthesia as a karmic undo-ment of the fact that, having run a sword right through him, I left him to die of his wounds instead of having the spiritual courage to kill him. In that case, I should have, out of mercy, put an end to it, but I didn't. So in this lifetime, I undid it. Let's see if that's a fact or not. "That's a fact: resist" (True). Yeah, that's a fact. So one will get recalls like that, and you can do spiritual research.

I think it's valuable to do karmic research to clear up any misunderstandings. One thing you can clear up with karmic research is self-pity. The idea that you're the innocent victim of all these vicissitudes of life—with a little karmic research, you will find that you are not the innocent victim of all these vicissitudes of life. No; that you have really chosen this. Well, it's a lot easier to accept the consequences of your own actions. You say, "Out of my willingness to evolve spiritually, to be worthy of heaven, to be worthy of God's Love, to experience the Infinite Reality of God"—you can respect yourself that you are actually willing to reincarnate and go through what you've gone through again as a human being for the mere chance of undoing it and choosing better. So you can respect yourself for what you've put yourself through. And you certainly have undone a lot of bad karma, so the worse life has been, the better it is, huh? If your life's been dreadful, boy, oh boy—I don't know how you rate. Well, I earned heaven, I'll tell you; I've been through quite a bit.

You could say, "If I chose this as an option, then why did I choose it? Because it says you're not forced to reincarnate." You don't have to, don't have to. It's an option. We can choose it. If you could skip the childhood part of it, you know, it wouldn't be so bad. This time, the childhood part was so boring, I don't know how I got through it. I thought children were awfully boring, and I used to look at them: "God, they're so dumb. They play these dumb games." I couldn't wait until I grew up. So I read Plato in the meantime while I waited to grow up. You weren't grown up until you were this high, and I was only this high, so I just had to sit in a chair and read Plato by myself. I thought childhood was quite boring. There wasn't anything particular in childhood I needed to undo. The disasters didn't start until later in life.

So you can see you may get a different position about your physical life this time. It might give you a different way to maybe respect yourself instead of kicking yourself. Instead of kicking yourself for errors, you might say to yourself, you can recontextualize it; that this was a different way of looking at it, a different way of learning, a different choice. And I turned it down this time. This time you turn down great wealth, let's say. You lost your shirt in the stock market. Oh, gee, high-tech stocks are just not the way to financial heaven, I guess, right? All of us live and learn. We try to gain what we can from this lifetime. We can turn this lifetime, no matter what, into a plus, to extract that which is spiritually valuable out of every iota of it. A lot of times, you can surprise yourself.

A guy stole a lot of money from you, let's say. You discovered that somebody embezzled a lot of money from you, and you want to get even. Well, it helps to find out that karmically, you embezzled a lot out of a lot of people, a lot of lifetimes. And it's payback time. That makes it a little easier to handle, right there, and to see that it doesn't really matter. So, the willingness to let every instant be the past, of course, closes the door to all regret about the past. And the way one's consciousness evolves, then, is the willingness to surrender everything as it arises. To live in the absolute, radical reality of the moment of "now" means, like listening to music, to let go of the last note and make room for the next. Each thing as it arises, you can let go wanting to change it. The willingness to surrender this instant to God as it arises means you don't live on the front of the wave, trying to anticipate the future; nor do you live on the back of the wave, trying to cling to the past. As it is now, it is spoken. As it is now, it is done. As it is now, it is acted upon. And you let it be the way it was, huh. Is that simple enough? It's walking on the edge of the knife. To walk precisely on the edge of the knife is what allows you to go through surgery without anesthesia, because the instant you begin to resist the pain, it becomes excruciating. It's only when you completely and totally surrender to it, not call it "pain," stop resisting, you become one with whatever the sensation is without any calling it anything—all of a sudden, one transcends it and the pain disappears as though being transported by angels to a different realm.

I wonder if that degree of surrender actually brings angels around, or something. "That's what happened: resist" (True). Okay. It was a definite sensation, as though one was being lifted out of the body by angelic beings. They're angelic because the exquisite grace, gentleness, and radiance of Love was profound. It was as if one was being lifted out of the physicality, and the physicality was going through all this surgery, and chopping off your thumbs and various things were going on. And there was only a feeling of infinite peace and joy. So, that surrendering, that intense surrender, then . . . well, let's ask that again. "The intensity of the surrender finesses the Presence of God expressed as the angelic: resist" (True). Wow, I didn't know that; suspected it but didn't know it for sure.

So you see, kinesiology, as we use it, is a constant learning tool. It's just a tool, that's all. It confirms, denies, tells you're in the wrong direction. It's like looking for Easter eggs—you're warmer, you're warmer, you're warmer—you know what I mean. You are warmer this way; no, this way, this way. And it sort of leads your investigation. Now karmically, you're beset by certain problems and questions in your life, so they tend to press for expression and for awareness. The past lives that probably are of any significance in one's life, most people already intuit them. They will start out as a joke—"Oh, some lifetime, I must have so-and-so"—usually starts out as a joke. They don't want anybody to think they believe in karma, so they say, "Well, some lifetime I must have been a pickpocket." I was a pickpocket in France one time. Anyway. I sort of knew that all along. You'll find that you sort of intuit, or people will mention to you, you know, "You're like an old farmer, for God's sake, the way you walk around and look down at the ground." You know, you just sort of knew you'd been a farmer a lot of lifetimes, you know what I'm sayin'.

It's like one is very close to consciousness. What's the value and the significance of it? The value and significance is that it may recontextualize your spiritual work in this lifetime in a way that is less painful, facilitate it, and broaden one's understanding of the evolution of consciousness itself. It's unlikely that you just came out of the blue, out of some kind of nothingness and appeared on this planet, calibrating at 430. I mean, it's just not a likelihood.

The other interesting observation is that without some kind of understanding of karma, there is no explanation of why it is that various individuals already have a calibrated level of consciousness at the moment of birth. How come this baby is born at 230, this one's born at 540, this one's born at 70? How would you explain that? A fickle God or careless God? I don't know. "I just roll the dice, and some fell off the table"? Little kids were born with AIDS and died of starvation by age of six months. What kind of karma is that, huh? Born with a calibrated energy of 30, which is not far from death. They're born half dead into a family with no resources, no money, no food, and all of them have AIDS, and they are terminal cases of tuberculosis—if the AIDS doesn't get them, the TB will. Or the nearest warlord will slaughter them anyway. How to explain this? How can you believe in a just God who determines all events as though He's arbitrary, and yet have people coming into the planet on all these various, different levels?

"Karma is the explanation why children come into this world calibrating at different levels: resist" (True). So, you see, you intuit the next step in your own spiritual evolution. And you use consciousness techniques such as kinesiology to affirm or deny them. Why? Because you begin to trust your own spiritual inspiration. The Presence of God within you expresses itself as spiritual inspiration, which is what leads you into spiritual pathways and attending lectures and studying books and doing mantras, and all that. That's coming from a spiritual intuition . . . inspiration. It's not personal, so you can't compliment yourself that you're spiritually oriented; nor can you attack yourself that you aren't.

Consciousness itself is impersonal. Everybody has it. Awareness is impersonal—everybody has it. The presence of the Self is ubiquitous in everybody. So it's not something you can rate yourself one way or the other. It's like you hear the call, and you become responsive to it. And now you become curious about spiritual matters. You become interested in overcoming defects, because your polarity is such in the gravity field of the Universe of God that you are attracted to the Light. Once one is attracted to the Light, one is attracted to the Light by virtue of all the spiritual decisions that have been made in the past, so that your karmic propensity now is to be attracted in this direction.

Most people who are seriously spiritually devoted accept that as normal and think, "Well, isn't everybody that way? Doesn't everybody want to go to church and give up sin and become a better person and go to heaven?" No. That is naive altogether. We see that 78 percent of the population prefers it the other way. They will consciously choose that which leads in the other direction. If given a choice, they will consciously choose it. That is also partly because of what they have been up to that point. So that you can't really berate anybody for what they are at this point, because what they are now is a consequence of what they have been. To many people it would seem that the option of a different choice is not open to them. If you're out at sea and shipwrecked at sea, it's not an option to drink pure water, because there isn't any. Many of the adolescents I see who come off the streets, a better choice is not really an option to them. It's not within their conscious options. You know, when you go to make a choice, you have a certain number of options. And these kids don't have these three options. You either fight and kill, or you're a coward and go down. So they've got one choice. They've got one choice. It doesn't dawn on them that they could leave their present environment. It's not a possibility. So it's almost as though the positive options themselves are earned. The positive option is not there unless you've earned the positive option, you might say.

The Spiritual Heart

According to Ramana Maharshi, the seat of the heart is in the right side of the chest. He was talking about the various levels of the aura which have different languaging, depending on the spiritual tradition from which you are speaking—in the Far East, or the Near East, or wherever. Anyway, he's apparently talking about a heart within the heart chakra as expressed in one of the sheaths. So I'm not aware of what he meant by it, and it puzzled many of his followers. Many people asked, and I forgot what his literal answer was. Let's see. We'll ask it today. I don't know what the answer is either. "What he meant was the spiritual heart: resist" (True). "That the spiritual heart is positioned in a certain way within the etheric body: resist" (True). "He's talking about the position of the heart chakra within the etheric body: resist" (True). "And that it's not concordant with the physical body: resist" (True). All right. So, he's saying it's not concordant anatomically with the physical body.

I only saw auras briefly in my lifetime, and it was with a lady who knew how to see auras. I said, "I can't see auras." She said, "Oh, anybody can see auras. Here, sit down." She told me how you see auras. She said, "Look right over the head there and don't focus on the head, and you'll see . . ." And then she showed me where to look and how to look, and by God, there *was* one. Well, I didn't know if it was just suggestion. Don't forget, I'm scientifically trained, you know, and I know a lot of suggestions. So I'm saying to myself, "Well, this is suggestion." So I thought, *I'll test her out.* For one thing, when I saw this aura, it was gray, like this, and it was very lopsided. It was not auras like they are in pictures—they look like halos, or something. This person's sitting there, and here's this gray aura, and it is way over this way, over his right ear. And I said, "Where do you see the aura?" She said, "It's way over his right ear." "Okay, I *am* seeing them." Well, your fantasy would be that everybody's aura looks very neat, like an artist's drawing right around the body, you see. The energy field was way over like that. I don't know. I'm just speculating on what Ramana meant by that. I don't think it was anything important. I forget whether he said to meditate on it or not, but I didn't get that it was of any critical importance.

CHAPTER 9

The Experience of One's Own Existence Is Subjective

How can you verify the validity of your findings, such as, I suppose, in kinesiology or whatever, or in one's work? That's sort of the hypothetical asking the hypothetical, so it's not really answerable in a radical, logical way. But the experience of one's existence is purely subjective, and there is no escape from subjectivity. So, to ask somebody for what might be considered objective—from a certain intellectual, hypothetical viewpoint—doesn't really have any reality even if it was answerable. Because the experience of myself, Susan, and the audience simultaneously is that we use a certain technique to verify the yes or no of various things, but to some degree, we already know the answer, and all we're looking for is some external verification for the purpose of demonstration, really, and for showing how this technique can be used to further spiritual progress and gain access to information. Don't forget that the information that we talk about in these lectures and write about, et cetera—most of it has never been known in the history of mankind. Not known, certainly, in a verifiable way. Maybe some shaman had a vision of it, or somebody had a hallucination of it, but nobody has really contextualized it in a totally comprehensible way so as to make it assimilable and verifiable. You see, if you get an answer that's outside of the expected realm or outside of possibility, it requires an explanation. And occasionally we get an outrageous response. Well, that doesn't mean the response is wrong; it means that you don't comprehend it. A lot of times, you have to completely rephrase the question. Sometimes the question is already begging the answer and you'll get a refusal.

It's funny, but Consciousness is extremely bright, and when you think you outsmarted it, you find you didn't get away with it. Many a time—and we did it one time in front of an audience, and I've cited this example before; when we asked, "Carl Jung's energy is over 520," we got a no. Well, we'd done it hundreds of times. I know what Carl Jung's energy is. And she couldn't understand it, and I couldn't understand it. Well, we said, "It *is*." Well, he's dead, so it couldn't be, could it? It said no. We said, "It *was*," and we got a yes. So it's just phrasing one word. "Carl Jung *is* over 520," obviously the answer is no, but we were careless because we've asked that question so many times. Now, the whole thing has to be internally consistent. In other words, if you spent a few weeks with us and saw us do hundreds and hundreds of things, you begin to see a fabric of truth form itself which is internally consistent. "At this time I've done over 255,000 calibrations" (True); "260,000" (True); "265,000" (True); "270,000" (True); "275,000" (True); "280,000" (True); "290,000" (True); "Over 300,000 calibrations" (Not true); "Over 290,000 calibrations" (True); "294,000" (Not true). Two hundred and ninety-four thousand calibrations. Well, if you've looked at 294,000 rocks and examined them under a microscope, you begin to get a feeling for geology.

When I first saw kinesiology, I had already gone into that infinite paradigm we call "nonlinear" and which, religiously, is called "the Presence of God." So when I first saw it, I was already seeing it from a different paradigm of reality. The whole audience was within the linear, Newtonian domain. What they saw was a local phenomenon, and what I saw was a nonlocal phenomenon. We both witnessed the same event. To me it was obviously the nonlocal answer coming from the nature of consciousness itself. And the rest of the audience saw it as the reaction of the body's physiology to a turnip. Some people thought— well, you know, they presumed—but it was very clearly a nonlinear, impersonal response. It has nothing to do with the questioner; it has nothing to do with the person who was being the subject. And it was obviously the connection between the invisible, nonlinear domain and the consciousness of mankind as it expresses itself through the nervous system. So instantly I saw what was infinite, nonlocal, impersonal, and was a response of consciousness itself to the presence of Truth. At first we called it "True versus False," but that is not correct. I think in *Power vs. Force*, we said it was "True versus False," but in *Eye of the I,* we corrected that. It's not "True versus False"; it's "True versus Not True." There is no opposite to truth. Truth is either present or not. If truth is present, then you go strong. If truth is not present because it has no existence— so, that which is not real has no existence. Consciousness therefore does not respond to it, because it is only a belief system in your head with no reality. So there is no such thing in the universe as "no-ness." There's either yes or the absence of yes. That's a very profound spiritual understanding, because it destroys the artifact of the polarity of the opposites. And we use as the analogy of that, when you throw the switch on, electricity is present in the wire. Electricity is either present or not present. There is no condition known as "offness." So the duality of the ego is that "off" and "on" are opposites. There is no opposite to God. There is no opposite to truth. There is no opposite to existence. So when I hit the duality at age three and got it literally resolved at maybe age 60, of "existence versus nonexistence," the fallacy of it made me laugh. There is only existence. And you can see the absurdity of asking whether "nonexistence" exists. Nonexistence is not an option just like absence is not an option, you see. Something is either present or not present. There is no condition called "absence." You know what I mean? We can't send "absence" into this room and fill it up. "After we all leave here, we will send in 'absence'"—"absence" has no existence. There is either "here-ness" or "not-here-ness," but there is no such thing as "absence." But the ego's belief in that which is unreal is the cause of the human dilemma: that there's an opposite to God and that there's an opposite to existence.

The nearest thing to nonexistence is oblivion. And to see that is to solve the ancient dilemma of the Buddhic fallacies. There's errors in all religions, and the one in Buddhism is the misunderstanding of the Absolute Infinite as Void. And in its mistranslation, the Void becomes a state to be desired and achieved by the pathway of negation. Actually, nonexistence is not a possibility. Voidness as Nothingness is not a possibility. Voidness as absence of form or content is the absolute reality. But if one believes that the absolute reality to be achieved is the Buddha nature as Voidness, as though Voidness is a reality condition, leads one into the state of the Void, and when you leave the body, you go into oblivion. Then, because that's not a reality, you cannot stay in it. Because you cannot stay in it, you find yourself back at age three in a little wooden wagon, stunned by the fact that you exist again. That's the fallacy of the Hinayana pathway, a certain branch of the Hinayana pathway.

The misunderstanding that that which has no existence can exist as nonexistence—you see the fallacy of it, even within the realm of logic. But when spoken by a guru with gongs, shaved head, incense, sitting on a tiger skin, one assumes this is the ultimate authority. One worships it, deifies it, and now it becomes sought after: God as nonexistence. That's an impossible koan. You cannot get past that one until—what did we say—850. At 850, you pass the doorway. Hmm. The purpose of all that is to try to unhook the power of positionality creating a duality, which is the block to enlightenment.

If you see that only existence exists, if you see that only heat exists, if you see that in the supposed gradations between light and darkness, there is only the one— and that is light, and that darkness has no independent existence; then you're halfway to enlightenment, because those are the great obstacles.

The Field of Awareness

If consciousness is not personal, what does it mean we earn the chance for better opportunities or for better choices? It's like consciousness is the field, the field; karma is still content. One has not escaped content yet. To go beyond karma means to have escaped the limitation of content. Consciousness is infinite context. It has no form, like the sky. Karma would be like a cloud. It still has form; it hangs loose within the sky; it's within the sky. So, karma then would be the consequence of one's spiritual decisions have an influence on the shape of the cloud, but consciousness is like the sky. The field of consciousness which is impersonal is unaffected by the cloud. Where the cloud goes in the sky will depend on its shape, size, consistency, humidity, barometric pressure, and many things, yes? You see, in the meditative technique to realize the Presence of God, one goes back from identifying with the content of consciousness to the field itself to realize that I am not the content of the mind; I am that upon which the mind is playing, see? It's like I am the receiver and not the notes of the music. The receiver remains the same no matter what music is playing on it. You all of a sudden jump from identifying with the content—I am those thoughts, words, images and memories—to I am That which empowers them to become known. So, you become the knower of the field. You become the witness. You become, at a certain level, the experiencer. Beyond the experiencer is the witness and the observer. The witness and the observer and the experiencer arise out of an impersonal field. You can realize these things are impersonal, because witnessing and observing is not within—you cannot shut it on and off at will. If it's who you were, you could shut it on and off, but it's not who you are. Behind the witness/observer/experiencer is an impersonal, all-prevailing field of Consciousness itself. Even consciousness is not aware of its own existence except for the field of awareness. So you stop identifying with the movie, and you begin to see one can witness the movie only because that upon which it is being projected is formless. So you withdraw your investment in identification of self as form and content of memory and experience. You see yourself as that which is beyond form, that you are the field upon which form reveals itself as form.

You witness that the Self is impersonal because consciousness doesn't shift, no matter what you think about it or say about it or try to do with it—it's just there. Through-out the day, if one is awake, you're conscious. How do you know you're conscious? Because you're aware that you're conscious. And awareness itself is also impersonal. Aware-ness itself is also impersonal. So, you go back through the substratum, you're going back to God manifest as exis-tence, the awareness of existence, and there you transcend temporality, because that quality which you sense has no beginning and no end. Eventually you get back to God not only as manifest but as Unmanifest. Out of the manifest, Unmanifest arises.

The Unmanifest is traditionally in Christianity called the "Godhead." Out of the Godhead of the Unmanifest arises God as Manifest, out of which arises the universe. That all makes sense as you—in meditation, one can withdraw from identification with the movie, to see that except for Consciousness, there would be no awareness of the movie and that Consciousness is what prevails. And the content of the movie is evanescent. Therefore, as one spiritually evolves, one is less and less prone to investing in that which is transitory. Because the transitoriness of that which is temporary becomes increasingly obvious. Every acquisition someday later will be a problem in dis-position. Everything you acquire, someday you will now have the task of disposing of. So you spend all day acquir-ing it; it will take you two weeks to dispose of it. All has to be reboxed, sold at garage sales, transported, wholesaled, retailed, willed to somebody. In other words, that which is transitory becomes less and less of value. Therefore, spir-itual work itself becomes more and more valued because one realizes its permanency. Once you have made a cer-tain spiritual decision and see through certain spiritual illusions, that which you see is permanent. That which you see has a profound effect on one's karma. There is a man who wrote a book called *Omniology*, and he gave, you might say, the anatomy of that which is of the nonlinear, as paradoxical as that may sound: that the spirit body has within it a sort of karma body. It would be like a computer chip. So the spirit, then, is like a computer chip, but the computer chip of a different domain in which everything leaves an imprint throughout all of time.

So when we do kinesiologic research, we can go anywhere in time, anywhere in place, and we can pull out information that nobody has had access to. Nobody has ever had access to most of the things we do. . . . In fact, on this stage a lot of times, we have asked things that nobody's ever asked and nobody has ever gotten an answer—nor, if they got an answer, would they have any way of verifying the truth of that answer. We asked, "Did Jesus Christ ever have previous physical incarnations?" Anybody ever ask that you ever hear of? I never heard of it myself. Came out of the blue. And it came out of the blue to ask it here and now. You know what I'm sayin'? Never thought about it. I don't know that it necessarily means anything, except it's another piece in a puzzle. When you put it all together about your knowledge of Krishna and Buddha and Christ and all the Great Ones, you begin to get a sense of what the spiritual reality of that entity is and how it impacts your life and how it impacts all of society.

The Infinite Potentiality of the Evolution of Humanity

Ken Wilber famously wrote *The Holographic Paradigm and Other Paradoxes*. My guess is, he would be in the high 400s as a consequence. "Ken Wilber, we have permission in front of this audience: resist" (True). "He is over 460" (True); "470" (True); "480" (Not true). He would be in the high 400s because that's very advanced understanding he has of the nature of the universe and how it operates, that it is a holographic unity. He also escapes the trap of causality.

Because this is on this [right] side of the universe, therefore this is where it is on this [left] side of the universe. But this [on the right] is not causing that [on the left] to be over there. You understand that? In a holographic universe, you see, things do not come about as a result of the ego's belief in causality. They come about as a result of the manifestation of Creation as it evolves into the providence of perception in what seems to be sequential. As Creation unfolds, nothing is causing anything. Understand? It's beyond causality. Each thing *is* what it is. And that completely answers. There's no questions to be answered. Each thing is totally that which it is and requires no cause. So, cause is really a tautology—it's really a hypothetical absurdity to say, "What is causing this?" It's the linear, Newtonian paradigm which presumes an invisible thing called "cause," just like it presumes behind thinkingness there is a thinker, behind doingness there is a doer, behind acting there is an actor. There is no actor behind the actor; nor is there a doer behind doingness. There is no thinker behind the thinkingness. There is no speaker behind the speakingness. Speaking is speaking of its own as the unfoldment of the potentiality, the infinite potentiality of the evolution of humanity, in consciousness as it is expressed in this entity. "That's a fact: resist" (True). Whew, I would hate to have found out *that* was not right! And repeat it with a correction! I would have to recall what I said. That is a fact, because each moment as speakingness is speaking itself—which is what it's doing—there isn't any "speakerness" behind it. There is no speaker behind the speakingness. The speakingness is speaking itself. Because the expression of life, then, at this instant in the gravity field of this audience, manifesting through this entity, speaks back to you as this speakingness because it's all happening spontaneously, you understand? Everything is happening of its own, as an expression of that which it is, which is why I don't sound like a bell. Because the voice box is what speakingness speaks through, see. But there is no fantasied, and therefore there is no cause behind what you see as the unfoldment of God as form.

I promised you I would unearth the fallacy behind Thomas Aquinas's proof of the existence of God through tracing back cause to first cause, one of the famous arguments. There's four of them. One of the famous ones is tracing back cause through a sequence of causes to find the prime cause. The idea is, if you trace back a bunch of billiard balls, you'll find *the* billiard ball that starts the whole bunch going. Except when you get there, there ain't no billiard ball there. There's a cue; oh, a cue stick—you won't find another billiard ball. So if you go from cause C, cause B, cause A, and look for the primary cause, you're not going to find any primary cause, because there isn't any primary cause there. What you find is *Source*. So, the fallacy of the argument is, if you think in an infinite sequence that you're also going to find another one of the same things. No. What happens is, it changes quality, changes quality. Let's take water. We'll use the thermometer. You see, at 212, water is a gas. Below 212, water is a liquid. Below 32, water is a solid. Well, we've got solid, liquid, and gas, and yet at the same time, it's all H_2O. The essential nature of water has not changed at all, but its quality has changed considerably.

The significance of the calibrated levels of Consciousness is because it's not just quantitative. It's true these are logarithms, but at each stage here, these energy fields which dominate consciousness changed quality. And therein lies both their blessing at the topside and their curse at the lower side. Because this may be only two points lower than this, but this one will kill you—changes its quality, changes its quality, changes its quality. It's the change of quality, not just the quantity. So the logarithmic numbers denote levels of power, but as they change, they change quality. So the nonlinear cannot be accurately described from the viewpoint of the linear. You cannot compare lead with platinum by comparing their atomic weights, because the quality of platinum and lead are completely different. Lead is relatively inert, whereas a milligram of platinum can catalyze tons of ore. You can get tons and tons of ore out of one milligram of platinum, because it doesn't get used up in the process. Lead is inert. You can put lead someplace, and it doesn't do anything for a few hundred years.

Your Level of Consciousness Is Set by Spiritual Decision

People have often asked me, does the level of consciousness fluctuate throughout the day? Well, we said that level of consciousness is set by spiritual decision. It's really the Spiritual Will that sets it, so consciousness is a little more stable than that. Emotions tend to come and go, but your level of spiritual commitment hasn't really changed. You say, "Well, I'd like to kill that guy, and he deserves to get beat up, and I hope he gets his." And then you say, "Well, would you do that?" "Well, not really." So, you were spinning off an emotion, but that's not who you really are. So we inherit an emotional body which becomes known to the world as your persona—personality, emotional body—but it's not the real you. It's sort of the evanescent play-interaction with the world, making learned, appropriate responses, et cetera. But it's not the real you, because the real you is when your life depends on it—what would you say in a situation, and you'd say, "Thumbs up," or "Thumbs down." Well, whether you vote thumbs up or thumbs down is going to make a big decision. So if the gladiator out there, the crowd says, "Thumbs up," or "Thumbs down," if you vote with the thumbs down, you join the karma of the crowd who chose his death for the sheer thrill of watching him bleed all over the sand. Done, thousands of times. You, on the other hand, could be the one who puts his thumb up, huh. If you do, you may get the fury of the crowd, so you're in a hell of a place. The crowd will kill you for putting thumbs up when they all put thumbs down. But if you put thumbs down, you join their karma. So very often, not infrequently, you're up against a spiritual or moral decision like that.

So that which interacts with the world is not intrinsically the Self, but it certainly reflects it. That which is activated on the stage right here is the persona. It's the learned part that knows how to verbalize, interact, express appropriately to get ideas and thoughts across, and it is not innately the same as the Reality of the Self which has no form and, frankly, doesn't say anything. If I ask my inner self what it thinks about all this, it doesn't think about it. Doesn't consider it thinkable, doesn't have thinkability. On the other hand, if something varies somewhat from the absolute truth of whatever this consciousness is here at the moment, it instantly lets you know. And the difficulty, as we said, up to 600, the kundalini energy pouring up your spine is exquisite and joy is exquisite; you're surrounded by infinite beauty and harmony; everything happens with synchronicity. When you think something, it appears. It's heavenly, and at 600, one is just immobilized by it. All of a sudden, the sense of the Presence is so profound that how the physicality persists is strictly up to the world, actually, because at that point, there's no interest in it. It'll stop breathing too. It stops all activity, and the bliss is all-prevailing; even breathing stops. And life goes right on if the universe—if the karma, I suppose, of the universe and the karma of the individual so decide, then the breathing will start because somebody comes by and stimulates it to breathe or gets you to eat again, or something like this. Otherwise, you'd just leave it. And I think we've found—what? Of those who hit 600, 50 percent do leave the body. Half of the people just let it fall over, and it's wonderful. Whether it stays or it doesn't stay is totally irrelevant. Then, beyond that, usually it stays there, but sometimes it goes up to 700. Or sometimes it will start from down below and then hit 700, and suddenly your consciousness is 700. That's Ramana Maharshi and Nisargadatta Maharaj, and, I presume, Muhammad. I don't know the story of Muhammad. Muhammad was only 700, but 700 is the world of the Sage and a profoundly enlightened state. Usually at 700, it just stays there. At that point you don't leave the mountain and you don't have many clothes. You can sit on a tiger skin and eat icky food off a palm leaf. Or you can get a job back in New York City, I suppose, and get real.

You know my sense of humor. It's funny, you know. It just says the most bizarre things. People will say, "You laugh at your own jokes." I tell them, "They're not my

jokes—I never heard 'em—they just come out of the blue."
They hit me as hilarious, frankly. I don't know where they
come from. Some of the funniest things have just come
out of the blue and they just knock me over, because I
have a sense of humor. It has nothing to do with me—I
didn't make it up. They're not my jokes. They just came
out of the blue spontaneously. So everything happens
spontaneously.

And then, from around 700, it usually doesn't change.
I don't know why it continued to change in this instance.
But from that point on, it is not blissful. Frequently, it's
extremely painful. One's sensitivity to the slightest out-
ness is exquisite. And, in case it bypasses your notice, the
aura reacts with intense pain, which was quite distressing.
And the pain often was severe and lasted for many hours
and days, sometimes, until you could find what the out-
ness was and correct it. And then it would go away. But
the next slightest thing, it would start it. I was lamenting
that—one time, I was lamenting and we were in Korea,
and Susan pulled a Buddhist bible out. See, in Korea in
the hotel room, you open the drawer and there's not just a
Holy Bible, Christian bible, but a Buddhist bible, you know.
She pulled out the Buddhist bible and flips it open. And
the Buddha was saying that he was wracked with pain and
beset by demons, and his bones felt like they were cracked.
Instantly, I felt better when I heard that.

See, even as I was speaking, even as I was speaking.
We will share with the audience the reality of how this
all works, because there's nothing mysterious about it.
As I got near speaking this morning, I felt a twinge out.
There was something. I could pick out . . . I could tell—
sense it was the third eye of the Atmic body. "There was
something out in the third eye of the Atmic body: resist"

(True). "It was a Luciferic energy: resist" (True). "It had to do with the spiritual ego seeing a gain: resist" (True). "The spiritual ego was attracted to the power of absolute certainty: resist" (True). The spiritual ego was attracted. It knew that the absolute power of absolute certainty is considerable, and the spiritual ego instantly went for it. I felt it go for it. It wants to seize the power inherent in being a transmitter of absolute certainty. Like the remnant of some entity wants to hang on to that, to come back through and reach out toward you from . . . from where, I don't know. Let's see. See, we learn instant by instant. I'm just showing how it actually works. "That spiritual ego was personal: resist" (True). "That's the remnant of the personal ego: resist" (True). "Which is attracted to the thought of power: resist" (True).

So you see, the spiritual purification is continuous. The more you learn, the more astute you become at perceiving its nooks and crannies. And you are after it all the time. After a while it's like the princess sleeping on the pea . . . you can feel the pea-under-the-mattress kind of a sensitivity. It's like the instant it comes up, you know there's something out about it. You instantly look to see what it is about it. From your knowledge of the ego, one could presume what is probably operating, and then with kinesiology, verify if that is so and choose the opposite— to be grateful for the Absoluteness of Spiritual Certainty. To choose that as the ultimate option.

That's the Luciferic energy I see. As you evolve, it's like some test comes up with it, you see.

Is there an end zone from all this? Is there an absolute end to spiritual evolution? In my understanding of the nature of God, no—that the evolution of consciousness is a foreverness. It's a foreverness. "We have permission to ask this: resist" (True). "It is a foreverness: resist" (True). Yes, it's a foreverness. So, there is no end in the sense of the limitation of beginning and end, which are concepts. Beginning and end are concepts of languaging and a definition; therefore, that which is Infinite would not be compatible with that which has a beginning and an ending. So, within Reality there are no endings because there are no beginnings. So, all measurement, then, is an arbitrary positionality of the ego, which says "this" is a beginning and "this" is an ending. It would just trigger the next sequence.

"The end times are a reality on this plane: resist" (Not true). No. "The end times are a reality on certain astral planes: resist" (True). Yes. The end times as seen in Revelation, as seen by many psychics, channelers, tarot card readers, are a reality on certain astral realms because people who have experienced it are very truthful when they're telling you the reality of what they experienced. They are very convincing. They did, indeed, experience that reality. But it was not this realm. The error was to presume that it refers to this planetary evolution, which it does not. It does, however, apply to certain astral realms. So, John calibrates at 70—the source of the book of Revelations. I think Revelations calibrates at 70. John was the originator, and Revelations was a hallucination, a very elaborated hallucination. He calibrated at 70, and the hallucination calibrates at 70. When you ask the source of that hallucination, it was one of the lower astral realms. Now, what John envisioned and experienced as a potentiality and envisioned reality for the future and all has been seen by lots of people. There are a number of people in Sedona, some whom I knew personally, who actually went to those astral realms, thought they were some kind of Divine

heaven, and came back with the message. Build under-
ground houses and wait for the end times, and California
will fall off into the ocean, and Phoenix will become a sea-
port. And so, many people did. The survivalists scattered
to the hills and waited for the end times. The year 2000
came and went, so they packed up. Did they change their
ways? No, they just changed the date.

I knew some of these people were telling the truth from
their experiential. Experientially, that is what they experienced. And they *did* experience it. And they *were* telling
the truth, because that is what they experienced, but it
was on an astral realm and it applies to an astral realm. It
does not apply to this realm. The karma of earthly existence is different than the astral.

There is an infinite number of astral realms, each with
their own hierarchy. There're semigods, there're demigods,
there're chieftains, there're masters—spiritual masters. They
all have strange names—usually "Master Kokilula, he's in
charge of 'this'; and then beyond him is Master So-and-So."
And beyond him is another realm, and beyond him is
another—so there's a whole hierarchy within the astral
domains, each one ruled by a demigod. They think they're
"God" god, but they are actually demigods. They're very
common in history. Historical mythology is full of them.
Anyway, the astral realms are current realities in certain
dimensions. One chooses those dimensions. In teaching
students, I tell them to avoid them. Not that they're not
intriguing; they are quite intriguing. A lot of them are
quite clever, and they have their own hierarchy. Some of
them even have Jesus in the hierarchy. Jesus is a part of
their domain, as far as they're concerned. But they're diver-
sions. And if you check with kinesiology and say, "Should I
go there?" you'll always get a no. And you can be intrigued

by it and sucked in by it and become influenced by some entity on the other side. So the way to handle entities on the other side is to ask what is their calibrated level of consciousness, as if they were in a physical body, and find out what is the level of consciousness that is being channeled, and what is the consciousness level of the channeler; and what are the intentions of both.

First of all, you don't need any information that comes from out of body. All the information of spiritual truth that you ever need to hear in a lifetime has already been spoken by those in bodies. There is no truth held by any entity on the other side, channeled or otherwise, who holds some truth that you need to know to reach salvation or enlightenment. There are no secrets in the universe. There are no secrets. Nobody is holding any mystical, ancient mystery knowledge that by manipulating certain symbols or something that you're going to accelerate, or you're going to bypass karma, or some of these outlandish promises they make. Transcend karma? Yeah, right. Because you're trying to transcend karma, you've just created new karma called "trying to transcend karma." You know what I'm saying. To get away from these footprints in the snow, you've merely created some new footprints in the snow. You haven't gotten away from leaving footprints in the snow. So I say that everything you need to know spiritually has been said, and it's being said in a live body.

What's Important Is Integrity in a Teaching

There are certain things that were taken by inner dictation, and when you calibrate the energy field, it's 600. Well, any teaching at 600 is worth following, whatever its source. Generally, though, you'll find they're in the high 200s. Most of the channelers and channeled entities are in the high 200s, no matter what titles they may tell you. It's always "Master Somebody" or "Baba Somebody," but they are all in the high 200s. There's nothing wrong with the high 200s, because what's important is integrity. Integrity is over 200. So it can be integrous ignorance. What is said is *so*, but it is not a very high truth. So, unless you can verify the truth of a teaching, I wouldn't bother following it; and what can be learned that you need to know? So, you'll find it's entertainment.

If you realize it's entertainment—and it probably has a certain reality within a certain narrow sense of what's real—then it's harmless, but I see too many people swept aside by that which is not so harmless and its purpose and intention is to deter you from the pathway.

The difficulty with that which has denied God— which is called the lower astral—is, it hates that which affirms God. You'll notice that as you go below 200, you get into levels of that which hates holiness, purity, and spits upon it. There're certain neighborhoods that will take you there; you just try being pure and see how long you last. It's despised. The leader of Cambodia, Pol Pot, any kind of affection or love was against the law. You could be executed for any display of any kind of a positive feeling; it was actually illegal to have a positive feeling or to express it. The Japanese in Manchuria, the same thing. To bayonet an innocent baby in the arms of its mother showed that you had achieved the ultimate: the hard, uncaring, cold-killer consciousness of that which denies God. So, the lower astral is full of entities who have made that kind of a decision. Wanting to adopt them as your spiritual mentor is not really the best advice.

Illnesses and Karma

When will a certain illness remit? In spiritual evolution, we said that karma plays a very heavy component. Having strangled a lot of people to death might delay your recovery from COPD in this lifetime—who knows? You know what I'm saying? Don't forget, the evolution of consciousness throughout time, it was at 190 for centuries, and before it was 190, it was much lower than 190. It was way back at 50 or 60 or 70. It was normal in those times to enslave or kill those you conquered. They weren't violating any social standards or doing anything immoral. So, when you look back at previous lifetimes, you're going to discover what life was like in those times. You can't contextualize it in terms of the year 2002. To execute one's captives was normal, expected; in fact, you got executed for *not* executing them! You understand? So, you have to have a certain context and understanding when you begin to do any kind of karmic research and realize what you're talking about is the entity that lived in times when living by your wits was the top of society. Royalty lived by their wits and nipped each other in the purse as often as possible, and in the bed in between. So you can hardly be surprised to find that the kinds of actions that may have had unfortunate karmic consequences in this lifetime, if you put 'em in the context of that time, weren't really all that bad, so as to prevent yourself from attacking yourself spiritually. It can be that in this particular lifetime, one won't allow a certain thing to heal until one feels one has achieved the karmic purpose of that and sort of finished it, you might say. So you might hang on to an illness—not consciously, but karmic propensity may see to it that it persists for a while.

"The pain in the nervous system from 800 and up is due to the fact that the human nervous system hasn't evolved to that level yet: resist" (True). "But it does as a consequence of the spiritual work: resist" (True). Well, questions arise constantly. People are growing and evolving and learning, and we do the same thing, and so we are always asking questions. Somebody asked, "Why do you think the evolution of consciousness becomes painful beyond a certain level?" It's great up to about 700; then about 800 it gets painful. And I've always intuited that the nervous system is not equipped for it and not evolved that far. It could be in a few thousand years, but at this point, the nervous system is not that evolved. However, as you progress in consciousness, the nervous system does begin to adapt to it. It actually strengthens; the nerves actually get thicker and capable of handling more spiritual energy.

Understanding Christ Consciousness

Has Jesus Christ ever physically reincarnated on the earth plane? "Jesus Christ has reincarnated on the earth plane: resist" (Not true). No, my own understanding of the second coming of Christ is that it occurred in 1986. The New Age people got really wild. There was a book, in fact, that Jesus Christ was secretly living in Brooklyn somewhere!

My understanding is that the human being, because he identifies himself as a physicality, expects that the second coming of Christ is going to be a physicality. My understanding of Christ Consciousness is that it's a level of consciousness. And what reappears and dominates the planet is Christ Consciousness and therefore, a physicality is really irrelevant and immaterial. In 1986, the consciousness level of mankind—probably has to do with the karma of human evolution—jumped from 180 to 207. When it jumped from that which is negative to that which is positive, to me, that's the real re-emergence of the Christ Consciousness. When that which represents Love, truth, and integrity prevails over that which is destructive and nonintegrous, to me, that's the return or the emergence of Christ Consciousness in the form of Consciousness. I don't know that somebody at the level of Christ would be interested in physicality. He might do it as a teaching tool. I myself wouldn't choose it, necessarily. I mean, you'd have to appear on TV. You know what I'm sayin', and all.

When Certain Things in Your Life Keep Recurring

Is delving into past lives helpful? Yes. We've tried to demonstrate it up here. You see, sometimes, mysteriously, strange things happen recurrently in your life. There's no rational explanation. There was one series of rather very strange kinds of events. They kept recurring . . . all were in different countries and different circumstances, and the same kind of thing would recur. I mean, I just knew there was something—I didn't believe in karma in those days, but I knew it was something on some other level. And I would tell my analyst about it, and he'd say, "It's just your paranoia. You're connecting this all together as a logical sequence, because that's a quality of the human mind." I said, "That's true." But statistically, that's very, very unlikely, you know, that these strange things would recur. Of course, later on when I did check it out karmically, then it just verified what I sort of intuited as a fact. Then the question is, "Now what do you do about it?" Well, you pray very intensely, and whatever the defect was in a past life that accounts for this, you refute it—declare one's choice of the opposite, dedicate one's life to the opposite. So, if you've been miserable toward little dogs . . . Let's say this lifetime, you're always getting bitten by dogs; you know what I'm saying. You begin to wonder, "Is there something about me? Do dogs hate me, or what the hell is it?" You can be in the middle of nowhere and a dog comes out of somebody's apartment and bites you in the leg. You begin to wonder if you were once cruel to dogs and tortured them to death, or something. It does make it more comprehensible.

When we were talking about causality and overcoming the illusion of causality, then I will just explain to you how I saw the universe when that state came on. The most shocking thing initially was not only the translucence and the Oneness of all things and the intensity of the Divinity that shone forth through all of Creation, but the awareness that everything was happening spontaneously as a result of its expression of its essence. Each thing is the perfect expression of its own essence as it manifests at this moment of Creation. Everything is happening spontaneously of its own. And if you see that, you get transported to a different realm. In this realm the illusion is that everything is creating something else from elsewhere. Everything is therefore dependent on something outside of itself. Everything is dependent on some external explanation for its existence, which misses the essence of Reality: that each thing is being what it is spontaneously because that's the way it expresses its essence at this moment in the context of these conditions. You understand? Is that comprehensible? Each thing is being merely what it is. I looked at the cat, and there sits this cat. And I was just struck with the profound perfection of its exquisite cat-ness. It's sitting there, 101 percent radiating cat-ness and not anything else. And that cat-ness is not coming from elsewhere. It is not dependent on anything outside of itself. But it's the unfoldment of its potentiality to be a perfect kitty, and as it sits there and purrs, it's perfection at that moment. It is being absolutely, 100 percent the infinite potentiality of kitty-ness at that moment, right? It's not dependent on anything outside of itself to be what it is. It's not dependent on anything outside of itself to be what it is. So, each one of us is, in the same way, free then to express the potentiality of that which we are as we are created in the context of our current karma and the conditions of the world, you know?

The Importance of Being over Level 200

The world went from 190 to the prevailing 207. That's extremely important, because in a balance, if it's one feather to this way [A] or one feather to this way [B], when you project out a laser beam an infinite number of millions of miles, you are quite a way from here [A] over to here [B]. You understand what I am saying? The slightest variation, when projected throughout the consciousness of all of mankind over eons of time, so the destiny of mankind is profoundly different than what it was. At 190, nuclear wipeout was almost inevitable. Potentiality. Because it's below 200, it has innate within itself the seeds of its own destruction. And in due time, it would have brought about its own destruction. The only reason it had not succeeded in totally destroying itself up to that time is that it did not have a powerful-enough weapon. Once mankind invented a powerful-enough weapon, 190 would have wiped us out. It would have wiped us out.

And so, "At the height of the Cold War, left to its own devices, 190 would have brought about the destruction of mankind itself: resist" (True). Yeah, 190, left to its own devices, like a locomotive with no control, would have run itself to death and run itself off the tracks. To go from 190 to 207 was already profoundly significant. Then we found, only very recently, that between book one and book two—or between book one and book three, I forget—that a percentage of people below 200 dropped from 85 percent to 78 percent. That's a huge drop; 7 percent, percent agewise, when you look at it across all of humanity, means that what was tenable in the past is no longer tenable to increasing proportions of the populace. For instance, we see all of Europe now forbids capital punishment—all of Europe. The only thing about capital punishment—aside from its spiritual obviousness—from a practical viewpoint, is if you make a mistake, you can't undo it. And now, with . . . what do you call it, karma testing and blood . . . ? DNA, yeah. Now with DNA, how would you sleep knowing you put somebody to death, and then you discover he was the wrong guy? I mean, I don't know. That would be pretty hard to live with. So it gives you no chance to correct an error, no chance to correct an error. All right.

So the implication, then, is quite profound: that the consciousness level of mankind is advancing. The number of people below 200 is diminishing. And the number of people over 600 has doubled or tripled. When we wrote the book, there were very few over 600, I think. Now we've got over 30. So, the consciousness of mankind is advancing. It seemed to me, up to the consciousness level of 190, that mankind was called *Homo sapiens. Homo sapiens.* In the evolution of the humankind, there was Neanderthal man and there was Cro-Magnon man. They all calibrated around 70. Then there was *Homo erectus.* And the hominid improved to where we now have *Homo sapiens.* The *Homo sapiens* calibrated at 190, up to the year 1986. And then the consciousness level jumped to 207—very, very critical, because it changes quality, just like water at 32 degrees Fahrenheit. Here it's ice and solid, and here it's liquid. So, consciousness at 190 changes *quality* when it goes over 200.

Now it seems to me, this signals the birth of *Homo spiritus*. *Homo sapiens* has gone as far as he can go. World War II was pretty much the end of that guy. We saw what *Homo sapiens* could do. He could create great inventions and great bombs and great bullets and great military machines. And what did he do with it? He used it to destroy innocent people. No, it seems to me that the birth of spiritual awareness level over 200 means that man, humankind, has now rebirthed as *Homo spiritus*. The spiritual significance and meaning of life is now what is constantly being questioned. It's even being questioned about, do we have the right to put people to death who are murderers? That's *Homo spiritus*—to even question what is the right of the accused mass killer, who would never have come up at the lower levels. You'd just execute the guy the next morning, and that would be the end of the story, wouldn't it? No questions asked. Although such a question can be taken to the political extreme of absurdity, the mere fact that it is given countenance in today's society means the birth of a new, greater, and more intense spiritual awareness, in which we are almost asking to be reborn from a moral viewpoint. What is the moral, responsible action to take? What is the moral action to take with a prisoner of war— and are they prisoners of war? It seems like the country is almost being confronted by a re-estimation of its moral values and the degree to which it is committed to moral values. So, it's almost like a rebirth of society. So, to me, it's the birth of *Homo spiritus*.

Spiritual Commitment Can Lead to Changes in One's Life

So, there are disruptions in one's personal life. Becoming spiritually committed can lead to very major disruptions. You can walk away from a very intense worldly commitment and just turn your back on it and drive off with an old truck full of a bunch of old tools, leaving it all behind—all the Oriental rugs and the antiques, and all that. Just walk away from everything, which leads some of your family members to decide that you're mentally ill or you're in a middle-age crisis, or you have just had a nervous breakdown, or you were always a little bit off. "And now he's really off."

Why do they say that? Because we've said these are two different paradigms of reality. The linear, Newtonian paradigm—the one of supposed-rational world of science, logic, and the intellect and the university—is one paradigm of reality. The nonlinear is not real, is not real to the Newtonian dimension; is not real. So, a person whose awareness is confined to being a one-eyed man thinks that the vision of a two-eyed man is bizarre, right? So in the world of the blind, the one-eyed man is king. But in the world of the one-eyed, the two-eyed man, again, is strange. So, to the person limited to the Newtonian paradigm of reality—they are like the one-eyed man, and as you become spiritually aware, it's like you have two eyes and now you see things in three dimensions, whereas they only see them in two. So, you ask the family members. They can consider you've gone off the deep end, but that's all right, because how do you explain it to loved ones? You really can't. "Ah," they say, "he's found God."

How do you develop tolerance for people as they are? See, everything and everyone is in a point of evolution, including one's own perception and spiritual growth, so compassion for the less fortunate—let us call the very bottom of the barrel the "less fortunate"—you have to see their actions as an impersonal manifestation of the human ego when it is unmodified by any kind of spiritual awareness whatsoever. It seems to have escaped spiritual awareness altogether. To do it in the name of God, of course, is what outrages everybody from the pope on down. The pope, you know, who calibrates about 570, which is perfect. The pope and the head of great churches—the most ideal calibration is about 570.

So, the head of a world church—you see, at 600, you're not much good as a head of a world church. You sit there blissed out, and you're not too functional. So, you'd be a nice figurehead to put someplace, and there are people who go and light candles to you and get your blessing, but you can't run a world church. Especially with the multiple decisions and implications of the international political . . . and the very exquisite and delicate spiritual decisions to be made. Because no matter what move you make, it influences millions of people, either adversely or beneficially from multiple levels, either economic or political or spiritual. So there's extremely difficult decisions to be made, and you really need 570 to do it. You need that much compassion, and you also need to be in the world to that degree. Now, at 700, people would say there is no such world; don't worry about it. The world of your perception has no reality, so don't bother worrying about it. Just perfect yourself, and that's all you can do. And that also, on a certain level, is true. The greatest gift you can give to the world is to perfect your own degree of consciousness.

Everything Is Perfect as It Is

When we say everything is perfect as it is, that has to be contextualized, because you could say, "Well, isn't the ego perfect as it is?" Well, it's a perfect expression of where it is at this point in time, based on this karmic propensity under the current conditions.

There's a mollusk at the bottom of the sea that's the most poisonous thing on the planet. If you examine poisons, you will find some interesting things. The black mamba has 14 different poisonous enzymes; any one of them is enough to kill you. There is a spider that has about 20 different poisonous enzymes, any one of which will kill you.

There is worse than that. There is a mollusk at the bottom of the sea who bores a hole in its victim and injects it with a poison which includes 40 poisons. Every one of those poisons is enough to kill an elephant, and it's got 40 of them. Now, would that serve any purpose from the viewpoint of evolution? No, because one killer neuropeptide destroyer, or whatever it is, is enough. It's got 40, so it's like a concentration of venom within one specific lifeform. We see that venom and that which is poisonous, then, is present on the planet. It always causes pain. It doesn't just kill you. Even the scorpion bite, you just don't go painlessly paralyzed; the pain is agonizing. So, there is that which calibrates very low; which is poisonous, instills pain, and its purpose is to kill; in contradistinction to that which is dedicated to healing, the relief of pain; and they're two contrasting ways to go. Therefore, each thing is demonstrating the essence of that which it is. You say, "Does it have a purpose?" No, because purpose is teleological thinking. Purpose is saying: because "this" seems to result in "that," that is the *purpose* of "this"—to cause "that." No, that is teleologic thinking, which is a logical fallacy: the error of *post hoc ergo propter hoc*—because a thing follows, therefore it's caused by, or it's the purpose, of it. All we're saying is that each thing becomes the manifestation of that which it is.

We're up in a small town, and a workman came up with a truck, and there in the back sat a little white dog. A little white dog got out of the truck and came over to greet us. And it just wiggled all over with happiness. Its tail was just going crazy, like *this*. It, like, falls in love with you instantly. It just fell in love with us instantly. It just radiated love, lovingness. It responded to love. It was looking for love. It seems to live in the world of love. It looks for love, thrives on love, gives love, reflects love, and the tail tells you. It just radiates that which it is. Now, isn't that strange that a dog at 500 is higher than a lot of human beings at 70? The dog kills nobody, kills nothing, brings comfort, joy, and happiness, and reflects that. And therefore I was surprised when I first calibrated the wag of a dog's tail and got it was 500. I said, "Whoa, that's higher than many of the people on the planet—most of the people on the planet." They won't approach you with trust, love, caringness; nor do they respond to love. Most people are scared to death of love, you know. You look at a person lovingly, with a prolonged, open glance, and a lot of people will shrink and get scared as ever. You try that at a stop sign in the city of New York, you'll get arrested. You look over at the car next to you with love in your face, and they call the police on the cell phone: "A killer—he's staring in my windows, officer." It would be totally misinterpreted, wouldn't it?

And I got the same kick when I noticed the kitty's purr. I calibrated the kitty's purr, and it seemed to be interested in love, looking for love, responsive to love, and seemed to live in a world of lovingness. So I can't answer you why love comes through an animal, except that we think of evolution in terms of intellect. We don't think in terms that lovingness could be evolved without the presence of an intellect. In fact, that which has an intellect is less likely to be loving than something that doesn't have an intellect, a lot of times.

Destiny Is Ultimately Perfect

When the soul manifests from the field of consciousness, does it carry a charge, either negative or positive, that can be termed the "karma" of the soul? Yes, I think that's specifically what we were saying this morning. The soul automatically, because of what it has become, is like a cork in water and automatically gravitates in the field of consciousness to that with which it identifies. And therefore, destiny is ultimately perfect. "That's correct: resist" (True). That's correct, yep. Automatically. So, the soul automatically gravitates to what it's attracted to, to that with which it is compatible. Just like the dog ran to love—if I hated dogs, I don't know, he might have shrunk off, or he might have tried . . . I don't know what he would have done. I should ask him.

CHAPTER 10

Aim for the Highest Level of Compassion

Two hundred is the dividing line between force and power; 540—is that the difference between ego and one's higher calling? Well, don't forget, these points are arbitrary—200 was not arbitrary; the calling it 200 was arbitrary. It was obvious that the world could be divided into that which makes you go strong and that which makes you go weak.

There is an interesting book called *Red World/Green World* by a lady named Margaret Chaney, and she said that there's Red people and Green people, and there's Red foods and Green foods. Well, she was just using that as a way of speaking. She's saying that people divide up into those which react positively to certain kinds of food and those which react negatively, and she grouped out two groups. There are the Red people—they respond with kinesiology positively to the following foods, and there's the Green people, and they respond positively to the following foods and they react negatively to the other foods. So her thesis was that Green people will get sick if they keep eating Red food all the time and can't seem to get well. And when they discover what they're eating is inimical to their health, they will regain their health. And now she's worried because a lot of medications are coming out in generic. So, the brand name—let's say you're a Red person—and the brand name tests Red, so you say, "Penicillin G is good for me, yes. I'm a Red person and that's a Red product, right? Okay, so it's harmonious with my energy," or whatever. Now they put out a generic brand of the same thing, only it tests out Green. So, now you're a Red person taking a Green pill, and this penicillin is not helping you. So she's worried about you—what are we going to do now? The generics are coming out, and they are coming out in a different category. So kinesiology can lead you into all kinds of conundrums, huh?

We just numerically called it 200 because that worked out as far as the logarithms go; 540 is the level of Unconditional Love. It just happens to be there. Love is at 500, and we say you can be very loving but still have conditionalities. When does Love become Unconditional? So, when Love is Unconditional, we found it calibrates at 540.

Christ Consciousness

Have we ever calibrated the level before Christ appeared and then right after Christ appeared? Let's see. "We have permission to ask this question" (True). "The appearance of Christ on the consciousness changed the overall level of the consciousness of mankind: resist" (True). "It raised it: resist" (True). "When we say 'Christ,' we mean the appearance of His teaching: resist" (True). "We don't mean the appearance of His physicality: resist" (True).

So, we're not talking about necessarily when the Baby Jesus sat there in the swaddling clothes, or something. "Before the birth of Christ, the consciousness level of mankind was over, oh boy, over 90: resist" (True). "Over 95: resist" (Not true). "Before the birth of Christ, the consciousness level of mankind as a whole was over 95: resist" (True). "96: resist" (Not true). About 95. Let's see, where's 95? Man lived in fear. "After the birth of Christ, the consciousness level of mankind increased: resist" (True). "Increased over 5 points: resist" (True). "10 points: resist" (True). "15 points: resist" (True). "20 points: resist" (True). "30 points: resist" (True). "40 points: resist" (Not true). "Just the physicality of Jesus Christ raised the consciousness level of man over 40 points: resist" (True). The physicality of the presence of Christ on the planet raised the consciousness level of mankind 40 points. "The teachings of Christ as they spread through the Roman Empire continued to increase the level of man's consciousness: resist" (True). "The spread of Christianity through the Roman Empire increased the consciousness level of mankind another 20 points" (True); "Another 30 points" (True); "Another 40 points" (Not true).

The birth of Christ as a physicality apparently was like a window to God and radiated that energy, jumped it 40 points, which is enormous. The teachings of Christ, then, radiated out, and were carried throughout the Roman Empire, and raised the consciousness level of mankind further.

The history of the evolution of the Roman Empire is quite interesting from the viewpoint of consciousness. Some of the Roman emperors were really quite advanced, almost more advanced than modern man, recognizing the equality of man; recognizing the right of the slave to a trial, a judicial trial; tolerance for all religions, except with the proviso that you also had to acknowledge the Roman gods. So, the Roman gods showed your allegiance to Rome as an empire and to the emperor, but so long as you did that, you could worship any gods you wanted. So it was pretty evolved. And it's interesting because it is the foundation of our Western culture. I think it helps advance one's spiritual awareness and consciousness because it increases your tolerance for that which differs from yourself—when you sort of become aware of how consciousness evolved and how the evolution of that consciousness expressed itself in cultures as they spread out across the world and the impact of the human experience. So, in a way, you're sort of owning yourself as the totality of mankind. There was certainly a period in the evolution of this consciousness of owning the self as the Self and totality of all of mankind. And so, understanding the evolution of humanity as culture and as it expresses itself over time can have a broadening effect and make one a little broader, which means less critical of that which differs from yourself, which makes the ego a little easier to transcend—because you sort of get off rigid positionalities as you become more sophisticated and see how consciousness evolved and expressed itself through the various religions and cultures. We become tolerant of that which is different than ourself. Of course, what we're shocked by is the egocentricity of it and the cost in society, but we can perhaps understand how it could evolve. So to be compassionate toward all of life means to be really, relatively sophisticated and educated about how consciousness evolved throughout time and then expressed itself in society in its various ways. As we said before, to understand society is to understand the ego. So, you are not wasting your time in studying history or sociology, because you're seeing how the ego outcrops itself . . . what do you call it? Out-something-or-other itself—out-something itself, out-pictures itself—how's that? How it expresses itself collectively. The collective ego, then, is the individual ego projected outward and expressed in human society on a grand scale where it's easy to see.

▲ ▲ ▲

[I was asked,] "You indicate that there were something like 294,000 calibrations. Are the results of those calibrations available somewhere to be a resource?" The book I'm working on now—well, I am finishing up *I*, the book *I*. The original manuscript was revised, and now I'm revising the revision. Then I will have to correct the revised revision . . . but in the meantime, during the intervals, the book I think I'm going to call *Radical Reality [Truth vs. Falsehood]*—in it we do about a thousand calibrations, going back through history—from Nero, Caesar, Caligula; through more recent history; through Nazi regimes; and into recent events, from Gorbachev to current rulers. I can give you examples. For instance, FDR was 499; Churchill was 510; most American presidents are in the mid-400s. Signers of the Declaration of Independence were about 510; the Constitution of the United States is 700. So, we can go back through the Magna Carta, we go through the evolution of democracy from the beginning of time. We calibrate theologians from the founders of the Christian church on down. We go through all the major events in human history; and current life, from MTV—it calibrates about 190—to computer games; and musicians—the great musicians, the popular musicians, and the classical musicians. The great classical musicians were generally in the 500s; some were higher. The great architects—we calibrated the great cathedrals of the world.

When I traveled in Europe, what attracted me was to go from cathedral to cathedral. They calibrate around 700, so you can see why they are attractive. To travel through the country of France and see Chartres Cathedral arising above the level of the hayfields way off in the distance is an unforgettable experience. So we do the great cathedrals and compare it, let's say, with the Crystal Cathedral currently in Los Angeles. We did all the major spiritual writers throughout history, of ancient and recent times, in the various books of the Bible and various things like that; various spiritual traditions and churches and teachers and gurus. We have pretty much covered all of human society. The scientists, the writers, the inventors, the great industrialists, current politicians. I think the highest calibration we got for a current head of state is the current president of Mexico. Surprisingly enough, the current president of Mexico calibrates around 560 or something, very, very high—the highest on the planet. And what does he talk about? He talks about cooperation, mutuality—see, he's not against winning and losing; he is not against make-wrong. He's not even into make-wrong. He's, "Here's where we are at and let's see how we can improve from there," so that everyone benefits. Well, that is a very advanced spiritual concept, that everyone benefits and with an idea of integrity and fairness and equality; and the same time, everything legal and cooperative. So a lot can be learned, and therefore I think it's a worthy enterprise.

The negatives, of course, in current society are rather obvious to anybody who's spiritually sophisticated at all. They hardly need calibration. Then we calibrated a lot of the great criminals, famous criminals of ancient times to find out . . . In other words, we're trying to get a topography of the evolution of mankind over recorded time. Where is Jack the Ripper? He's at 70. Where's Bin Laden? He's at 70. Where is a dinosaur? A dinosaur is at 70. The instinct of the dinosaur and the instinct of this person are the same. Jack the Ripper dismembers and rips to death its prey. I mean, it's almost identical; it's almost like a dinosaur spirit got into a human body, you know what I'm saying? I begin to wonder—is there a crossover? So anyway, it's an interesting work in that we are trying to develop a topography, a different dimension of understanding human consciousness and its expression as society, from Heinrich Himmler in World War II to Vicente Fox in today's world.

We did a lot of movie stars, famous singers, songs, and find out what their general range [is], and then there are exceptions. Louis Armstrong, way up in the 500s. The capacity to be loving at all times and in all places apparently was the characteristic.

So, it's just interesting, because you learn things because you see everything in a different dimension now. And as you see the calibration, you get, "Oh, I see. I get . . . oh, yeah, I see." It's like you get greater depth spiritually in comprehending the totality of human evolution, which in the net effect is to develop a compassion for it, as almost an experiment of creation. It's almost as though the evolution of life on this planet is almost an experiment—to see where, if you let it loose without any guidance or controls, what does it do? It ends up as a mollusk at the bottom of the sea that creates 40 enzymes at one time. And it also creates saints—the same life, but is it the same life energy or a different one, you know what I'm saying? That leads to rather profound questions.

The Karmic Shift of Mankind

Who was responsible for the massive shift in 1986? I've never fully investigated it. I just assumed that the collective positive karma of mankind had crested at that level. It happened to be at the time of the Harmonic Convergence. It happened to be at the time when Gorbachev pretty much pulled the blocks out from underneath the Russian USSR, atheistic empire. It was also the time of other major events which were concomitant. You see, when you go beyond causality, then you see that, let's say, a positionality here can radiate forth in the world of manifestation in multiple ways without one thing here necessarily being the *cause* of this. In other words, a positionality which surfaces in this way, it doesn't mean that the dissolution of monolithic Communism was *caused* by anything outside of itself, but it occurred at the same time. There is undoubtedly more to the story. We'll ask it in a general way. First of all, I know there's more to the story. "There's more to the story: resist" (True). Thank you. My own feeling was that it came from higher dimensions as a result of the consequence of positive accumulated karma of mankind. "That's correct: resist" (True). Well, we won't go into the details of it. It would be as though the collective karma of mankind as a whole had reached the point where it had crossed that collective.

Perhaps the last great finale of negativity was really World War II, in which the negativity, satanic energy, was massive. That caused almost a shock, but then, into the shock came that which was really more Luciferic in that it was seeking power rather than destruction—in the form of Communism and the USSR, which was really seeking power although it took expression as cruelty, and Stalin really was responsible for more deaths than Hitler. Nevertheless, it more or less ran its course. And of course, it was Gorbachev—if you calibrate Gorbachev's heart chakra, it's extremely high—so Gorbachev pulled the correct stops out, and the thing collapsed of itself without a shot. Gorbachev did not fire a shot. So, the West with all of its brave talk about "the war against Communism"—it was not the *war* against Communism that defeated Communism. It was the stops were pulled out by Gorbachev. Let's see what Gorbachev's heart is at. "We have permission: resist" (True). "Gorbachev's heart is over 540: resist" (True); "560" (Not true); "550" (True).

Wow. So, those people like Gandhi and Mandela and Gorbachev, people who changed all political history, their power came from a heart chakra at 550 and over. That is encouraging, because then it means increasing one's own capacity of lovingness has the capacity to undo the negativity of the world. In fact, it has the capacity to collapse whole empires. That which collapsed the USSR was the radiance of the heart chakra of one man.

However, that one man also represented something else that we write about, and that is when we talk about attractor energy fields. We say that each of these energy fields has an attractor pattern behind it. That brought us to describing what we call "critical factor analysis," one of the values of kinesiology. Many interacting systems are so complex, they are not capable of comprehension by the human intellect, nor by an assisted computer. A computer is limited to the Newtonian paradigm. It cannot be programmed for the nonlinear, by definition. Consequently, it can only mimic the intellect; it cannot mimic human intelligence. In any case, some situations are so enormously complex, they are beyond comprehension. This is a problem run into by big governments historically. The complexity of running a Roman Empire was staggering and, in the end, it just fell of inertia. All the soldiers just married the local girls and settled down and quit the army, and that was the end of the Roman Empire. No army could defeat the Roman Empire. It was the most formidable army the world has ever seen. It was unconquerable. And the Roman legions ruled all of Europe and the Mediterranean for a thousand years; it was [an] army invincible that ruled for a thousand years, and what brought it down—the kiss of a lovely woman. The soldiers all around Hadrian's Wall and all over the place met the local girls, fell in love with them and got married, and said, "The hell with it," and went to farming, and that was the end of the Roman legions.

In any complex situation, there is what I call "the critical factor." In a giant clockworks, if you know where to touch the giant clockworks, you can stop the entire clockworks by knowing precisely; the clockworks is so complex that even a master watchmaker can't figure it out. The same with an engineer. You see a locomotive running down the track with a hundred cars behind it—there's an enormous amount of force. But if you know where to touch the control in the cab, the engineer's cab, if you know where to touch it, you can stop the whole freight train. And so, if correctly positioned, then, knowing which of the pick-up sticks to pull out, the whole thing collapses; but you have to know which one. Gorbachev was there and Mandela was there. Each one was in a certain position. They also had a certain amount of power, because each one of them calibrates around 550. In all of them, the power emanates from the heart. So the power of Love, then, is transformational. As we saw with the birth of Christ, it jumped the calibration level of mankind 40 points, just the physicality being here, and it jumped another 40 points when His teachings began to cross the Roman Empire, and it totally changed Europe— the future of Europe and Western civilization—for all time.

So, an Avatar is one whose teachings and birth and presence recontextualized the significance of all of life, for all of mankind, throughout thousands of years. That's who we call an "Avatar." It's not the same as like the Avatar Used Book Company that you see running around town.

Avatar—I always get a kick out of people using the word *avatar* in the advertising of some program or something, because they don't understand what Avatar is. Avatar is of such enormous power that it changes all of mankind for thousands of years henceforth. It is the ideal by which everything else is measured. Every action of mankind, every court decision, every headline in the newspaper is unconsciously, if not consciously, measured according to the teachings of the Buddha or Christ or Muhammad or so. Muhammad calibrated at 700. You see, Buddha was 1,000; Christ was 1,000; Krishna was 1,000. All the great enlightened, fabled gurus of ancient times—Zoroaster at 1,000. Muhammad I've repeatedly calibrated at 700, so there was not the enormous power of spiritual truth to overcome, let's say, the tribal proclivities of that part of the world, perhaps, so the teaching breaks through—it breaks through. But don't forget, it broke through in Christianity also in the middle. Certainly, the end times being positioned. The truth of Christianity has broken through by some primitive negativity and savagery, which expressed itself in that way. And now we see it sort of delayed in the coming from that part of the world.

So, the spiritual person now is confronted with how to contextualize and comprehend and understand the current world events, but then again, it has been that way since I have been on the planet. World War I had just expired, and then came the Great Depression, and then World War II, and I don't know how many wars since then. And so, we're always confronted with the spiritual—the *seeming* spiritual dilemmas of the expression of the ego, in its expression as the actions, collective actions, of society.

In any case, all any of us can do is within our own heart to reach the highest level of compassion and

understanding and try to recontextualize it compassion-
ately, because in so doing, we undo it. So each of those who
were able to undo great negativity did so because in a way,
their heart was supported by the hearts of all of us. They
just didn't reach 550 all by their lonesome, out there on an
ice floe, you know. So, the evolution of the consciousness
of mankind is dependent on all the contributions of all of
us. So, each one of us counts, and each one of us counts
quite decisively. Each one of us certainly counts quite decisively. "That's a fact: resist" (True). You know, I've always
been suspicious of holy-sounding religious teachings, you
know what I'm saying. Holy-sounding religious teachings,
you say, "Yeah, right." I want to see, is that a fact, or is that
not a fact?

The Harmony of the Universe

There's the question of where astrology, for instance, fits
into this whole picture. Well, if the universe is one karmic whole, one karmic oneness, then all that's within the
universe, including its physical expressions as the planetary systems, et cetera, is part and parcel of that harmony,
huh? Therefore, the planets are also in harmony with
that universality. I would see it that, from a high level—
we've said that archangels calibrate 50,000 and up, and
you realize that we're talking about logarithmic progression here—one archangel at 50,000 that even thinks of
you is likely to knock you out of your body for some 20 or
30 years. And you're lucky to breathe again. Well anyway,
so from some very higher level of Divinity, then . . . let's
say, if everything is the interaction of energy fields, which
can be represented symbolically as an attractor field, that
means that all things are therefore in harmony. So, I don't

see a constellation as causing something within human experience on this planet. I see a third factor out here. Because of this third factor, this constellation is in this position and this event is happening commonly within the human experience, but this astrologic position is not causing the human experience. Both the human experience and the astrologic positionalities are expressing. So, if it is the time for great harvesting, let's say, that which is supportive of life in all of its expressions is expressing itself astrologically this way and has greater crops on this planet at this time, right? And then, at a later time in the cycle, the harvesting goes down and the astrologic position at that time is different.

So, to explain the harmony of the universe, which is consistent with the concept of the holographic universe and also the nonlinear dimensions of reality, it isn't that "this" on this side of the universe is *causing* "this," but it is concordant; and those of you who are familiar with advanced theoretical physics know that the spin of an electron on . . . and the spin of an electron in another part of the universe—this one is not *causing* the spin of this electron, but if this one stops and reverses, so does this, but there's no connection between the two of them. Which means that which you want to call "cause" is really just a terminology, a verbalization and a concept, and not a reality. But if you want to say there is a cause, the cause would then be outside both the electrons and that which causes this electron to go this way and this one, this way. So, this electron is not causing this. So, to me, an astrologic position does not *cause* pots and pans to break, but the timing of pots and pans breaking is simultaneous with that but not caused by that, you understand? Simultaneity does not mean causality. Just as peace appearing on the earth and all people praying for peace—it doesn't mean necessarily that the praying for the peace is *causing* the peace. But the appropriate time is an appropriate time for all things. And the appropriate timing of peace appearing and the appropriate time of praying for peace are probably simultaneous but not causal.

Some Spiritual Sayings Are Not Accurate

There are a lot of sayings, you know, spiritual sayings that are not exactly accurate. I mean, if they were all accurate, everybody would be enlightened. A lot of them are greatly inaccurate. To say, "All things are possible with God," is usually a hypothetical statement to counter somebody else's argument in order to prove that you're right. In usage, when looked at exactly, it cannot be so, because that which God cannot be is "not God." "All things are possible with God" is usually used to explain or give some kind of reification of the potential truth of something preposterous and quite unlikely. However, there is a correct usage to it within the infinite power of God in another context, in another sense . . . No, it's still not true. Because of the nature of creation itself that each thing becomes the essence of its own potentiality as the fulfillment of its own karma, there can't really be the fulfillment of something else's karma, or a bird would turn into a toad. No, a toad can only become a toad. So, we could say that that which "is" cannot become that which it is not. It can only be that which it is. That has to do with the self-identity of reality. The most difficult thing to see about in the enlightened condition—let's say, the radical sense of "I"—the thing that makes it the most difficult to understand is that everything is radically only that which it is.

It sounds like a nonsensical statement, but the ego cannot deal with anything except creating—cannot make any statement without creating a duality, thereby negating the reality of that which it is attempting to describe. Even the word *is* is incorrect. The radical reality of that which sits and speaks through this is-ness here is beyond is-ness; it is beyond beingness. Even a transitive, intransitive verb is incorrect. There is neither a subject nor a predicate. There is neither a "this" doing a "that," nor a "here" as compared to a "there." Those are all positionalities within mentalization. Those are all mentalizations. No such thing can be. The only thing that's possible is the reality of the cat being absolutely, completely, 101 percent cat—not caused by anything extraneous to itself. The only absolute statement of truth that's possible is the word *I*. To say "am," the suffix "am" to "I," is already a negation of the reality of the truth of "I," "is-ness," and "beingness," because the radical reality of that which I am is beyond either "is-ness" or "beingness." It is beyond existence or nonexistence. All such terminologies are mentations. So the most difficult thing about seeing the truth of the reality of who you are is the radical identity of the self as the Self. That which you subjectively experience as Self is that and nothing else. Then the ego comes in and tries to destroy that realization by adding all kinds of adjectives, adverbs. "I am that I am" is already deviating from truth. "Am-ness," "beingness" itself, is beyond the radical reality of the truth of that which you really are. Any verb at all is varying from truth. In fact, any noun is already varying from truth, because each one is adding something that is not essential to its essence, to that essence, and thereby blurring the recognition of the radical reality of its essence. To add the word "am" after "I" is already in error; it's already off the point.

Choice: Choose the Highest and Least Selfish

I think what we all tend to do is try to make what seems to be the highest decision, that which is most beneficial and loving, et cetera. We all try to make a decision which is, in our view of it, the least selfish. We try to choose "win-win" over "win-lose." At the same time, we try to clarify our perception of the conditions about which we feel we have to make a decision—whether we're seeing it in terms of "either/or–ness." We try to clarify in our inner mind, so it's very complex what our motivations are. A simple thing like, "Should I pick up a new kitty at the animal shelter?" can already be quite complex. On the other hand, it can be quite simple because each and everything, if examined to the full elaboration of which the ego is capable, becomes extremely complex. There's a much easier way to do it. "It's a good thing to get a nice kitty at the pound: resist" (True).

We know that having a pet increases longevity. It decreases heart attacks, drops people's blood pressure. I see a lot of depressed people in the office, and I always ask them, "Do you have a pet at home?" "No." Hmm. Well, we know that the presence of a pet increases longevity. We know that they're therapeutic. We know that they're very useful in nursing homes. The nursing homes I liked the best were ones that had dogs running around. If the nursing home didn't have a dog running around, it had a lower vibration. It did, really. And those which had Christian denominations running them seemed to have a higher energy and vibration. And there were always friendly dogs running around. So again, it isn't that this caused that, but a higher level of spiritual awareness, whatever, resulted in greater kindness on the part of the staff, a higher healing rate. And the presence of the dog—you can't say the dog caused the higher healing rate, but that which chose to have a dog there saw the importance of love to healing. And any health-field people who see the importance of love to healing are very likely to be more capable of bringing about healing in their patients. So every decision, then, can be seen, of course, from multiple viewpoints. And that which is most loving is undoubtedly probably what dominates most of the people on the field of spiritual inquiry. Of course, nowadays we can calibrate a thing too, but that doesn't mean it has to rule you.

You know, calibrating things is just verification; it's just verification. It's extremely useful. It's extremely useful as a research tool. The strangeness of this particular consciousness here was that it went through a whole great variety of experiences within the levels of consciousness, and it happened in a person with a scientific, medical, psychiatric, and psychoanalytic background. So that the curiosity of the intellect then was—the physician looked at it and said, "What in the world is that physiologically going on with the body?" The psychoanalyst wanted to look at it. So, the self-examination that went on was from the viewpoint which is not exactly traditional. And the description of the state then was expressed in a form that expressed the background of the entity. So *Power vs. Force*, then, was coming from the awareness that the scientific world, the world of the Newtonian paradigm, is ruled by logic and reason and science. So, how to present it, then— first as a Ph.D. dissertation to a university faculty where it would meet all the strict requirements of a Ph.D. doctoral dissertation—so, it was first presented there, to the most skeptical academic community to pass muster there before it went on and began to express itself in the nonlinear domain. So what I tried to do was create a crossover for that great block at 499. The great majority of spiritual seek-ers are in the 400s and cannot seem to break through that 499 into the 500s. How to make that bridge comprehen-sible was really the purpose of the work and the purpose of the lectures. Certain spiritual information is transfor-mative because it has within it, innately, such powerful energy that merely to hear it already transforms con-sciousness. So there is the commitment on the part of this entity to state all these statements that should be made, knowing that to merely hear that statement is itself of sig-nificance. And we'll stop very shortly. "The consciousness level of this community here sitting is over 435" (True); "440" (True); "442" (True); "444" (True); "445" (Not true).

Four hundred and forty-four—what were we at, 431? We went from 431 to 444. That's what we did as a com-munity today. We went from 431 to 444 as a result of just recontextualization of your own spiritual understanding— just from the material itself, you understand? 431 to 444. The average lifetime consciousness advances five points. So to go from 431 to 444—13 points—so, that's a quite enormous jump. We did that collectively. We did that col-lectively. On a certain level, we all own each other. We all own each other's consciousness. We're all responsible for each other's consciousness—not in a codependent way, but in understanding of the unity of the consciousness of mankind. Every endeavor that each one of us makes to get what was just said, it is helping everybody to get what was just said. My endeavor as a teacher is to try to make it as comprehensible as possible and defend the good name of God in the process, who has been much maligned by religion and other people and needs a friend. God needs a friend. God needs a friend in all of us. Every kind word is the glory of thanking God for our existence.

Your Intention Is the Most Profound Instrument

Any of those things which follow structure and form tend to be in the 400s. Don't forget, you are talking about a tool; you're not talking about the ultimate truth that may be revealed as the use of that tool. So many spiritual practices may calibrate in the 200s, but it would be like calibrating the level of a shovel, you know. With a shovel you can build the Taj Mahal, so you can't say a shovel is a weak instrument. You can build a Taj Mahal or you can dig your grave, so the shovel is not the whole answer. So, the consciousness of the person—let's say, any particular technique that you've learned—and almost everybody in this room has been around the block a little bit with different techniques, different teachings, different schools, different consciousness teachers. The intention, the commitment, the intention of the seeker is the most profound instrument. So, a person who is profoundly committed to God and digs with a small shovel will get further than a person with a small commitment but a major capacity for intellectual curiosity. Don't forget, the intellect itself is greedy, and many people have many books and have not moved much in their level of consciousness, so you have to begin to suspect that one is suffering from intellectual greed. The idea of having read everything and met everybody and known everybody, and met every guru on the planet, and all, in itself becomes an addiction. All you have to do is understand the absolute truth of one sentence, and that's sufficient. All you need is one sentence. And so, I say all spiritual work can start anywhere. You can pick out any place, because you can unravel the whole sweater from any place on the sweater, isn't that correct? And if you're willing to be forgiving—that alone—all you have to do is be willing to be forgiving everything and anybody, including yourself and everybody else, no matter where in time or space, including all of history, and you are already there. So, you don't need anything complicated.

CONCLUSION

✳

We hope you've been enthused and inspired by this book, which was transcribed from Dr. Hawkins's lectures presented in January and February 2002. This book set the stage for Dr. Hawkins's evolving and life-changing work, that encourages, educates, and invites every spiritual aspirant along the path to Enlightenment. Trust the Truthfulness in what you have read, put the ideas into practice, and with intention you can realize the Divinity that is within you and that is the Power of *who you truly are*.

Here are some of the main Truths for you to contemplate and understand as you go through your day:

▲ On the calibrated Map of Consciousness®, from 1 to 1,000, level 200 is the critical level.

Above 200 is that which is pro-life, supports life, and that which is true. Below 200 is that which is not true, does not support life; everything that is venomous, hateful, selfish, greedy, and destructive to others.

▲ The Map of Consciousness®, is not showing a duality of good and evil. There are gradations of Love. What we call *evil* is merely totally unloving.

▲ There is only one variable. The only variable between light and darkness is there is only light. There isn't light and darkness. Light is either there, or it's not there. The light can be very bright, or it can be very, very dim. When it gets very, very dim, we say it's darkness.

▲ Certain bits of information have an immense value. Just to have heard it, to get it, jumps you ahead enormously.

▲ Causality is a major roadblock because it blocks the awareness of the Presence of God, and the purpose of consciousness work is to discover the Presence of God within.

▲ To see through the illusion of causality, there's nothing causing anything out there. Nothing is causing anything else. What you see are *conditions*.

▲ What holds up spiritual progress is resistance. The main resistance is the narcissistic core of the ego and its belief in its own sovereignty. Becoming enlightened is really overcoming the claim and the domination of the ego to maintain its sovereignty.

▲ How do you surrender the ego? First, contextualize what ego really is, that it's not evil and that it's the persistence of the animal; but persistence of the animal deters one's spiritual evolution and therefore, the object is to transcend it. The best way to transcend it is to describe in some detail the actual mechanisms of the ego. For example, the ego's attraction and addiction is to the juice it gets out of suffering and being mistreated.

▲ Radical truth means you've got to take the mask off everything and be willing to see it for what it is, and now handle it from the viewpoint of emotional honesty.

▲ The way to reach enlightenment is quite simple. First, one chooses it.

▲ The subjective reality about which we're speaking, is in the split instant of now, the split instant of now is the source of the joy of your own existence.

▲ Because of your Love of God your consciousness grows. As your consciousness grows, it benefits all of mankind. Every living entity on this planet benefits from every single degree that your consciousness advances.

Dr. Hawkins often told us that through the repetition of the information given through reading and listening, a deeper understanding can occur. Read this book over and over again, or watch or listen to the lectures that are available, and profound insights will appear.

Gloria in Excelsis Deo!

APPENDIX

* ✳ *

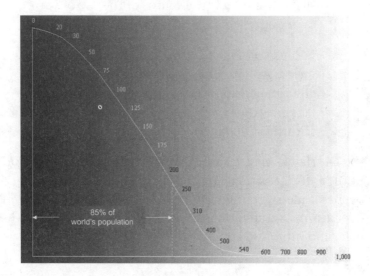

ABOUT THE AUTHOR

❋

David R. Hawkins, M.D., Ph.D. (1927–2012), was director of the Institute for Spiritual Research, Inc., and founder of the Path of Devotional Nonduality. He was renowned as a pioneering researcher in the field of consciousness as well as an author, lecturer, clinician, physician, and scientist. He served as an advisor to Catholic and Protestant churches, and Buddhist monasteries; appeared on major network television and radio programs; and lectured widely at such places as Westminster Abbey, the Oxford Forum, the University of Notre Dame, and Harvard University. His life was devoted to the upliftment of mankind until his death in 2012.

For more information on Dr. Hawkins's work, visit **veritaspub.com**.

Hay House Titles of Related Interest

We hope you enjoyed this Hay House book. If you'd like to receive our online catalog featuring additional information on Hay House books and products, or if you'd like to find out more about the Hay Foundation, please contact:

Hay House LLC, P.O. Box 5100, Carlsbad, CA 92018-5100
(760) 431-7695 or (800) 654-5126
www.hayhouse.com® • www.hayfoundation.org

———

Published in Australia by:
Hay House Australia Publishing Pty Ltd
18/36 Ralph St., Alexandria NSW 2015
Phone: +61 (02) 9669 4299
www.hayhouse.com.au

Published in the United Kingdom by:
Hay House UK Ltd
The Sixth Floor, Watson House,
54 Baker Street, London W1U 7BU
Phone: +44 (0) 203 927 7290
www.hayhouse.co.uk

Published in India by:
Hay House Publishers (India) Pvt Ltd
Muskaan Complex, Plot No. 3,
B-2, Vasant Kunj, New Delhi 110 070
Phone: +91 11 41761620
www.hayhouse.co.in

———

Access New Knowledge.
Anytime. Anywhere.

Learn and evolve at your own pace
with the world's leading experts.

www.hayhouseU.com